kosher by design
brings it home

picture-perfect food inspired by my travels

By **Susie Fishbein**

Photography by John Uher

Published by **ARTSCROLL / SHAAR PRESS**
4401 Second Avenue / Brooklyn, NY 11232 / (718) 921-9000 / www.artscroll.com

Distributed in Israel by **SIFRIATI / A. GITLER**
Moshav Magshimim / Israel

Distributed in Europe by **LEHMANNS**
Unit E, Viking Business Park, Rolling Mill Road / Jarrow, Tyne and Wear, NE32 3DP / England

Distributed in Australia and New Zealand by **GOLDS WORLD OF JUDAICA**
3-13 William Street / Balaclava, Melbourne 3183 / Victoria, Australia

Distributed in South Africa by **KOLLEL BOOKSHOP**
Northfield Centre / 17 Northfield Avenue / Glenhazel 2192 / Johannesburg, South Africa

ISBN-10: 1-4226-1689-4 / ISBN-13: 978-1-4226-1689-5

Printed in Canada

DEDICATION

This book is dedicated to **ERIC AND NAOMI GOLDBERG** of Naomi Boutique Tours & the team at **THE JEWISH JOURNEY** for introducing me to the culinary glories of international travel. I have been inspired by your thinking and your sense of adventure.

and

To my family — My greatest love and appreciation to my adorable husband **KALMAN** and my incredible children, **KATE, DANI, JODI,** and **ELI** — there is no one I'd rather see the world with and there is no one I'd rather come home to.

THANK YOU

To **JOHN UHER, MELANIE DUBBERLEY,** and **MAX LAU** — This one, like all of them, was a team effort. I am so grateful to have had you play on my team.

To **DEVORAH COHEN** and **ELI KROEN** — To each of you, thank you for your skillful eye and pleasant, elegant touch.

To **FELICE EISNER, KAREN FINKELSTEIN, ELISA GREENBAUM, TOVA OVITS,** and **JUDI DICK** — Wear wood eye bee with-out you? Thanks for your perfectionism in proofreading the manuscript.

To **GEDALIAH ZLOTOWITZ** and the **ARTSCROLL FAMILY** — For your unconditional support of all my endeavors.

To **GLADYS ESTRADA** — Usted es la mejor!

To all of the **CHABAD HOUSES, SHULS, SCHOOLS, SYNAGOGUES, JCCS, CHARITY GROUPS,** and **OTHERS ACROSS THE COUNTRY** that have brought me in for cooking demonstrations and shared their beautiful communities with me.

and of course, to **HASHEM,** for all of my blessings.

INTRODUCTION

What a delicious voyage it has been! The release of the original **Kosher by Design** (eight books and 480,000 copies ago) launched me on a never-ending book tour. I have made appearances in almost every state in the United States and in many parts of Canada. I have loved seeing how Jewish people live in all these different places. I have been warmly welcomed into hundreds of synagogues, homes, schools, bookstores, JCCs, and supermarkets. I have met thousands of wonderful fans and signed tens of thousands of books, some so worn and used they were falling out of their binding and held remnants of Shabbat meals long ago enjoyed. I have posed for photos, heard your wonderful stories, and been inspired by your enthusiasm for the cookbooks. I have watched, over 15 years, as food has become a media superstar. I developed an appreciation for the subtle differences in regional cooking in this country, and I picked up great recipe ideas here and there all along the way.

In the past six years, I have accepted international engagements. I have worked in Israel, France, multiple parts of Italy, and Mexico. This has been life-altering for my cooking world. In America, the current trend is fusion, cross-culinary mash ups — informed inspiration to put a new spin on an old recipe concept. It is fun and modern, and I love being inventive in the kitchen. The starkest contrast to that is what I discovered and was jolted by in European kitchens. Italian cooks value the safeguarding of their culinary traditions. The landscape of farmhouses, olive groves, architecturally perfect ancient hill towns that have been almost unchanged for hundreds of years, all lend themselves to maintaining the heritage. The Tuscan method of combining fresh vegetables with wild and cultivated herbs is almost ritualistic. Cheeses crafted on the pasturelands of the Po River, vinegars aged in barrels for decades in Modena, olives harvested and pressed into oil in Sorrento, pizza dough tossed high into the air in Naples, are all made in the exact same way as they have been for generations.

Food traditions are celebrated and fiercely guarded. In Northern Italy, foods like Goose Salami have their own festival days! Southern France is no different. Provence is the fruit and vegetable basket of France, and its centuries-old tradition of open-air market days remains a gastronomic ritual, almost untouched by modern times. Menus are based on what is found at the market that day. Produce is so fine that preparations are simple. Villages in Provence are places of such rare beauty that they have even been captured in the artwork of Van Gogh and Gauguin. When I worked with French and Italian chefs, they wanted to teach me the recipes exactly how their *Mamies* and *Nonnas* made them. These chefs cooked pure, clean, unfussy food. Their kitchens didn't even have pantries. Almost everything we cooked came fresh from a field or a farm. A real celebration of simple ingredients.

My favorite place of all to explore edible delights is in Israel. Israeli chefs combine both styles of cooking sensibilities. Israel is a combination of Old World and New World cuisines, with the Old World being diverse. Moroccan, Eastern European, Yemenite, Egyptian, Iraqi, Persian, and Turkish spoons all stir the pot of Israeli cuisine. This Israeli generation has seen the development of chefs who rival chefs throughout the world. Most do not come from a tradition of great culinary artists but rather from mothers and grandmothers who cooked and told stories about foods they inherited and places from their history. They passed them on to keep them alive. Talk to any great Israeli chefs, even those who have been trained outside of Israel, and in their hearts they are carrying their Yemenite grandmother or Moroccan mother and their family recipes, which greatly influence what they cook in a modern way today. We, as home cooks, greatly benefit from this. One can travel through an Israeli kitchen using a passport of spices.

The seasoning palette of Middle Eastern cooking is so varied in taste and color from the standard spices that I used to rely on so heavily. I have found them to be exciting, bold, and a healthful way to liven up my repertoire.

Moving out of the comfort zone of my New Jersey kitchen has been monumentally influential on my recipe writing. From the wonderful people I have met, to the generous chefs I have worked with, to the exciting new ingredients that stow away in my luggage, I have gained wisdom from the adventures and I am much richer for the experiences. I can't wait for you to see where this culinary road takes me next.

As I "bring home" the **Kosher by Design** series, I am humbled and amazed by the success of the books. Thank you for being on this journey with me and for making it the triumph that it has been. There has not been a day that I don't thank Hashem for the blessing of loving what I do. While travel is truly one of life's pleasures, and there is a thrill and gratification to seeing the world, there is nothing like the comfort found in **bringing it home**.

Susie Fishbein

PLEASE NOTE: D P M RESPECTIVELY REPRESENT DAIRY, PARVE, AND MEAT STATUS OF THE RECIPES.

Making kubbeh, Tel Aviv, Israel

Sombrero stand, Cancun, Mexico

Market day, Aix-en-Provence, France

Grape harvest
Terra di Seta winery, Tuscany, Italy

New Jersey

Starting out and heading home

Contents

Capri, Italy

Eight-Ball squash
New Jersey farmers market

Grilling vegetables, Israel

Market day, Provence, France

Tabun — a native pita oven, Israel

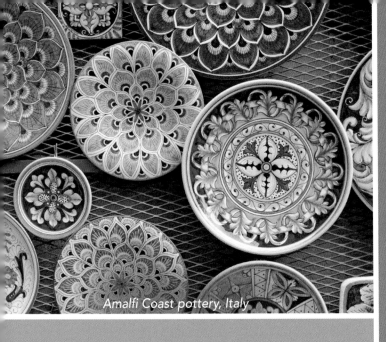

Amalfi Coast pottery, Italy

Beach scene, Cancun, Mexico

Appetizers

QUINOA mushroom *sliders*

Whenever I have to fly to a cooking demo show, I travel the night before. This allows me to take care of all flight delay worries, get a good night's sleep, and start the day in the town, where I will prep for 5-6 hours and then do the show. The day of any show is action packed, with no real break for breakfast or lunch, so I take along a healthy and filling dinner for the plane since it needs to hold me for a while. These appetizer sliders are my go-to in-flight meal. The quinoa provides protein and the veggies really fill me up.

 OR Ⓓ   YIELDS **12-14 SLIDERS**

1 cup quinoa; *if not pre-rinsed, rinse in a fine mesh strainer (see page 108)*

2 whole zucchini, *halved, seeds scooped out, cut into chunks*

16 ounces cremini mushrooms, *sliced*

6 cloves fresh garlic

3 tablespoons olive oil, *divided, plus more as needed*

2 teaspoons dried oregano

2 teaspoons fine sea salt

1 teaspoon freshly ground black pepper

1 teaspoon dried basil

1 teaspoon dried parsley

3 large eggs

½ cup all-purpose flour

½ cup grated Parmesan, *optional for dairy meals*

2 tablespoons canola oil, *plus more as needed*

12-14 slider buns

chummos, *for serving*

In a medium pot, bring the quinoa and 2 cups water to a boil. Turn down to a simmer; cook, covered, for 15-18 minutes, or until the quinoa pops. You should see tiny spirals (the germ) separating from and curling around the quinoa seeds.

Place the zucchini into the bowl of a food processor fitted with a metal "S" blade. Pulse 10-20 times, until the zucchini is chopped into shreds. Add the mushrooms and garlic; pulse until nicely chopped but don't pulse to a paste. Transfer to kitchen towel or a few layers of double length and doubled paper towels; squeeze out as much moisture as possible. If using paper towels, divide the zucchini mixture between 2 sets of paper towels.

Heat 1 tablespoon olive oil in a large nonstick skillet. Add the mushroom mixture. Sauté for 10 minutes, or until the liquid has cooked out and mixture is fragrant. Season with oregano, salt, pepper, basil, and parsley. Mix well. Sauté for an additional 5 minutes. Remove to a large bowl. Add the cooked quinoa, eggs, flour, and cheese, if using. Mix well with a gloved hand.

Wipe out the pan. Heat 2 tablespoons canola oil and 2 tablespoons olive oil in the pan. Using a ¼-cup measure, scoop out rounded portions of the mushroom mixture and drop into the pan; do not press down. Once the bottom is browned and seared, 3-4 minutes, flip it with a thin metal spatula or fish turner. Press lightly to form the patty. Cook until golden on the second side, 3-4 minutes. Serve on a slider bun with chummos.

petit FARCIE

In the spring of 2014, I worked in Provence, the garden of France. In stark contrast to fast food and giant supermarkets in this country are the outdoor markets of Provence. These markets have remained unchanged for generations and express the traditional French values of quality, freshness, and presentation of food. Miles of gorgeous vegetables, fruits, colorful spices, and beautiful textiles line the streets. The vitality and enthusiasm of buyers at these markets were a real spectacle for a tourist like me. Petit Farcie is a local specialty, although as I travel, I see a version of this stuffed vegetable dish in almost every culture.

 YIELDS **8 SERVINGS**

8 medium, firm plum tomatoes

6 Eight-Ball *or* other round zucchini

2 baby eggplants

4 baby bell peppers

1 tablespoon canola oil

½ red onion, *peeled,
    cut into ¼-inch dice*

4 cloves fresh garlic, *minced*

1 pound raw Merguez sausage, *NOT
    cured; see note on facing page*

1 teaspoon dried oregano

¼ teaspoon salt

¼ teaspoon black pepper

⅓ cup homestyle unflavored
    breadcrumbs

1 large egg, *beaten*

extra-virgin olive oil

Preheat the oven to 400°F. Position rack in the center of the oven. Trim off and set aside the top third of the tomatoes, zucchini, eggplant, and peppers, to use as caps. Cut a thin slice from the bottom of the vegetables that don't stand.

Using a VegiDrill or melon baller, carefully scoop out and discard the ribs, pulp, and seeds, hollowing out the tomatoes while keeping the outside intact. Repeat the hollowing-out process with the zucchini, eggplants, peppers, and any other vegetable that you are using (such as onions, patty pan squash, etc.). Place the vegetable shells into an oven-to-table baking dish coated with nonstick cooking spray. Set aside.

Heat the oil in a large skillet. Add the onion; cook until shiny, about 4 minutes. Add the garlic; cook over medium-low heat, stirring occasionally, until the onions are soft, 10 minutes. Transfer to a large bowl. Add the Merguez, oregano, salt, and pepper to the bowl. Knead well with your hands. Add the breadcrumbs and egg. Knead again. Season with salt and pepper.

Fill the vegetables with high mounds of stuffing. Roast, uncovered, for 25 minutes, until the meat is cooked through. The tomatoes are softer and should be removed earlier. Put the tops on the vegetables; roast an additional 10 minutes (5 for the tomatoes) until tops are beginning to crisp and the meat is sizzling. Remove from oven. Drizzle with olive oil. Serve lukewarm.

Eight-Ball squash are perfectly round squash that debut at local farmers markets throughout the summer. They make for a stunning presentation, but standard zucchini will taste just as good.

Merguez sausage is popular in Europe and is often a combination of lamb and beef. If you can't find it, you can use ground lamb seasoned with cumin, cayenne, garlic, and fennel. If your butcher sells the sausage in links, use 5 links and cut the meat out of the casings.

roasted EGGPLANT
with silan techina

Eggplant in some form or another can be found on every restaurant menu in Israel. Halved roast-ed eggplant is the ambassador of these appetizers. Gorgeous, simple, and healthy, with its smoky aroma and smooth cooked center, it is the perfect starter. Roasting the eggplants on the open flame adds so much flavor but can be a bit messy; make sure to cover the grates with foil to catch the charred skin — or follow this recipe for an oven-baked version.

 YIELDS **6 SERVINGS**

SILAN TECHINA

1 cup raw tahini *(sesame paste)*

⅓ cup fresh lemon juice

4 cloves fresh garlic, *minced*

pinch kosher salt

¼ teaspoon ground white pepper

½ cup warm water, *plus more as needed*

¼ cup silan *(date syrup)*

ROASTED EGGPLANT

3 large, long eggplants

⅓ cup olive oil

salt

pepper

pomegranate seeds, *for garnish*

radishes, *sliced paper-thin on a mandolin, for garnish*

scallions, *thinly sliced, for garnish*

Prepare the silan techina: In the bowl of a food processor fitted with the metal "S" blade, purée the tahini, lemon juice, garlic, salt, pepper, ½ cup warm water, and silan. You may need a bit more warm water to thin to desired consistency. Set aside.

Prepare the roasted eggplant: Preheat the oven to 400°F. Cut the eggplants in half lengthwise, cutting straight through the green stalk. Using a small sharp knife, make 3-4 "X" marks to score the eggplant flesh without cutting through to the skin.

Place the eggplant halves, cut-side up, on a baking sheet lined with parchment paper. Brush them heavily with olive oil. Sprinkle with salt and pepper. Roast for 35-40 minutes; the flesh should be soft, flavorful, and nicely browned. Remove from the oven; allow to cool.

Transfer the roasted eggplant to a platter or plates for serving. Drizzle on the silan techina; garnish with pomegranate seeds, radish slices, and scallions.

PITA BREAD *with green techina*

This recipe came to me through a really fun group cooking boot camp right outside of Machane Yehuda, called Te'amim. The chef, Udi Shlomi, claimed that the slapping down of the dough helps to form a pocket. Even if it doesn't, this step is a load of fun, especially if you shout "l'chaim" as you do it. Even if a pocket doesn't form, the pita will be delicious!

 YIELDS **15 PITAS**

PITA

6 cups all-purpose flour, *divided*

2½ cups lukewarm water, *divided*

2 tablespoons instant dry yeast *or bread machine yeast*

1 tablespoon sugar

2 teaspoons salt

½ teaspoon baking powder

GREEN TECHINA

2 cups fresh parsley leaves

3 cloves fresh garlic

1 tablespoon olive oil

2 cups *(17.6-ounce jar)* raw tahini *(sesame paste)*

1½ cups cold water, *plus more as needed*

juice of 1½ lemons

salt, *to taste*

Prepare the pita: In a medium bowl, whisk 1 cup flour, 1 cup water, yeast, and sugar. Cover with plastic wrap and let rise in a warm spot for 15 minutes. Place remaining 5 cups flour, 1½ cups water, salt, and baking powder into the bowl of a stand mixer fitted with the dough hook. Add in the yeast mixture; knead to form a dough that pulls away from the sides of the bowl. It should be smooth and no longer sticky. Cover; let rise for 1-2 hours, until doubled in volume.

Preheat the oven to 500°F. Line 2-3 cookie sheets with parchment paper.

Flour your work surface. Knead the dough and divide it into 15 balls the size of tennis balls. Flatten balls with rolling pin into ¼-inch thick circles. Slap the dough down with some force onto prepared cookie sheets; this helps form the pocket. Make sure the oven is at the hottest temperature.

Bake for 3 minutes; then flip each pita and bake until golden for another 2-3 minutes. Remove to a towel-lined bowl or basket; cover to steam and keep warm.

Prepare the green techina: In the bowl of a food processor fitted with the metal "S" blade, pulse the parsley, garlic, and olive oil; process for 2-3 minutes, scraping down the sides as needed.

Add the tahini and 1½ cups cold water; continue pulsing. Drizzle in the lemon juice and salt. Add more cold water, if needed, to thin to desired consistency. Serve with pitas.

CHICKEN pasta *genovese*

Chef Pepe owns Il Buco, a famous restaurant in Sorrento. For one glorious week, he cooked kosher for Naomi Boutique tours and I was permitted to learn over his shoulder. One of his crowd favorites was this dish, which is his grandmother's recipe. It tastes almost like a chicken soup gravy over pasta. I was happy to see that Chef Pepe used De Cecco brand pasta, not handmade pasta, for this dish. He did flour and deep-fry his own onions, but the packaged ones stand in as a convenient time-saver.

 YIELDS **6-8 SERVINGS**

⅓ cup extra-virgin olive oil

1 carrot, *peeled, cut into short, thin slivers*

1 stalk celery, *very thinly sliced*

2 medium onions, *peeled, cut into quarters, sliced*

1 medium red onion, *peeled, cut into quarters, sliced*

5 dark meat chicken quarters, *with bone and skin*

salt

pepper

⅓ cup fried onions, *French's or other brand*

¼ cup dry white wine

2-3 cups warm chicken stock

1 pound paccheri pasta, *or large tubes, cooked al dente according to package directions*

Pour the oil into a large (8-10-quart) pot. Add the carrot, celery, white onions, and red onion. Mix well. Place chicken on the bed of vegetables. Season with salt and pepper. Turn heat to medium. Bring to a simmer.

Turn heat to low; cook for 2 hours, uncovered. Using a wooden spoon, stir the chicken a few times during cooking. Make sure the onions are not browning, just gently cooking. Cover; cook for another 30 minutes. Remove the chicken; add the fried onions and wine. Simmer the sauce for 10 minutes, uncovered. Turn off the heat.

When the chicken is cool enough to handle, discard the skin and pull off as much of the meat as possible. Place meat on a cutting board; chop the chicken, leaving some pieces coarsely chopped for texture.

Return the chopped chicken to the pot. With gloved hands, knead the chicken mixture in the pot to really mix it all together. Return the heat to a simmer. Add the chicken stock, stirring until blended well. Serve over the cooked pasta tubes.

ARANCINI

Nothing goes to waste in a real Italian kitchen. When working with Chef Giuseppe Aversa on the Amalfi Coast, having leftover risotto at dinner was greeted with joy as we quickly turned it into arancini (rice balls) for lunch the next day. The arancini are so delicious, it is worth making the risotto, and I give you the recipe. If you have leftover risotto, this recipe is a snap to make.

 P OR **D**   YIELDS **6-8 SERVINGS**

¼ cup olive oil

½ **medium white onion,** *finely chopped*

6 **cremini mushrooms,** *finely chopped*

fine sea salt

ground black pepper

½ **pound** *(about 1¼ cups)* **Arborio** or **Carnaroli rice**

¼ cup **dry white wine**

3-4 cups **warm vegetable stock**

¼ cup **warm marinara sauce,** *plus more for serving*

½ cup **frozen peas,** *blanched in boiling water or microwaved for 2 minutes in water, drained*

2 **egg yolks**

2 **leaves fresh basil,** *finely chopped*

canola oil

all-purpose flour

4 **mozzarella sticks,** *each cut into 5 pieces, optional for dairy meals*

4 **large eggs, beaten**

1 cup **fine unseasoned breadcrumbs**

Heat the oil in a large, wide pot or Dutch oven over medium heat until shimmering. Add the onion and mushrooms. Season with a pinch of salt and pepper; cook, stirring occasionally, until the onion has softened, 5-6 minutes.

Add the rice; cook, stirring constantly with a wooden spoon and making sure to scrape the bottom of the pan, until the rice starts to toast, 1-2 minutes. Add the wine; cook, stirring occasionally, until all the liquid has been absorbed.

Add the stock, a ladle or two at a time, along with a nice pinch of salt, to cover the rice. Stir, allowing it to bubble. Lower the flame. Over the course of 18-22 minutes, as it cooks out, continue to add stock to cover the rice. It will simmer and absorb the stock. Keep topping it off, stirring every few minutes. At this point the rice should be tender but still a bit firm to the bite. Stir in the warm marinara sauce. Simmer for additional 2 minutes, scraping the bottom of the pot with a wooden spoon. Remove from heat. Taste; season with salt and pepper as needed. Stir in the peas.

Transfer the risotto to a rimmed baking sheet and spread it into an even layer. Let it sit until cooled to room temperature, about 30 minutes. Cover with plastic wrap; refrigerate until chilled, at least an hour or overnight. Mix in egg yolks and basil.

Fill a Dutch oven or a large, heavy-bottomed pot halfway with oil; heat over medium-high heat until it reaches 355°F on a deep-frying/candy thermometer. This can also be done in a deep fryer.

Meanwhile, set up a jellyroll pan and shake some flour into it. Moistening your hands with water as needed to prevent sticking, roll about ¼-cup portion of the risotto in your palm to form a smooth, compact ball the size of a ping-pong ball. You will make about 20 arancini. If making dairy, flatten the ball slightly, press your finger into the center of the rice ball. Insert a piece of mozzarella, pinch the rice around the filling to enclose, and roll into a ball. Place into the floured pan and repeat with the remaining portions of risotto; set aside. If making parve, just roll the ball tightly.

Set up a breading station with 3 bowls: One with flour seasoned with salt and pepper, one with the beaten eggs, and one with the breadcrumbs. Working with 1 risotto ball at a time, roll it in the flour until lightly coated, tapping off any excess. Then dip it into the eggs, letting any excess drip off. Finally, roll it in the breadcrumbs until evenly coated. Return it to the baking sheet. Repeat with the remaining risotto balls.

When the oil is ready, add some of the breaded balls and fry, turning occasionally, until golden brown all over, about 5 minutes. Using a slotted spoon or spider, remove the arancini. Sprinkle with salt. Repeat with the remaining breaded balls. Serve immediately, 3 to a plate, with the warmed marinara sauce.

coconut *lime* **PARGIYOT** skewers

Thai flavors come together beautifully for this stunning appetizer. It is fine at room temperature, so it would make a great Shabbos lunch starter or buffet item. Since the chicken is dark meat, it does not dry out the way some white meat cutlet dishes do when held over.

 YIELDS **6 SERVINGS**

6 boneless, skinless chicken thighs *(pargiyot)*

1 cup coconut milk, *stirred well*

1 tablespoon soy sauce

1 tablespoon honey

3 cloves fresh garlic, *minced*

1 teaspoon minced fresh ginger

zest of ½ lime

juice of 1 lime

¼ teaspoon red pepper flakes

12 cremini mushroom caps

2 tablespoons canola oil

1 avocado, *peeled, pitted, cut into ¼-inch dice*

1 ripe mango, *peeled, pitted, cut into ¼-inch dice*

1 (15-ounce) can black beans, *rinsed and drained*

2 tablespoons chopped fresh cilantro leaves

8 fresh basil leaves, *chopped*

juice of ½ lime

2 teaspoons extra-virgin olive oil

¼ teaspoon fine sea salt

In a 1-quart container, using an immersion blender, combine the coconut milk, soy sauce, honey, garlic, ginger, lime zest, lime juice, and red pepper flakes. This can also be done in a blender.

Transfer mixture to a ziplock bag. Add the chicken and mushroom caps. Marinate in the refrigerator for an hour.

Cut each chicken thigh in half widthwise. Thread a mushroom cap, folded chicken piece, second mushroom cap, and second folded chicken piece onto a skewer. Press the skewer through the stem end of the mushrooms through the top to avoid splitting them.

Heat 2 tablespoons canola oil in a grill pan until very hot but not smoking. Lay the skewers into the grill pan so they all fit. Sear for 5-6 minutes per side, trying not to move them around until it's time to flip them to the second side.

Meanwhile, in a medium bowl, combine avocado, mango, and black beans. Stir in the cilantro and basil. Drizzle with lime juice, olive oil, and salt. Spread onto platter; arrange the chicken skewers over the mixture.

CHICKEN lollipops
with ranch dip

A few Passovers ago, I worked for Ram Destinations at The Ritz Carlton in Cancun, Mexico. I loved working with my sidekick Sergi Flaster and Chef Carlos Garcia, who ran their culinary center. I picked up some nice Mexican dish ideas, which you will see in this book. But when I was not working, I was eating like a queen. One of my favorite dishes was at a "bistro" restaurant that they staged — chicken lollipops with a ranch dip. Their lollipops were deep fried and delicious. You can do this if you are serving immediately; otherwise, the skin gets soggy. Also, these days, I am trying not to deep fry foods that can be made in another way, so I came up with a grilled marinated lollipop recipe to go with my version of the dip.

  YIELDS **12 LOLLIPOPS**

CHICKEN LOLLIPOPS

12 chicken drumsticks, *prepared as lollipops, see note on facing page*

4 tablespoons hot sauce

3 tablespoons canola oil

1 tablespoon apple cider vinegar

1 teaspoon ground black pepper

1 teaspoon cayenne

1 teaspoon salt

1 teaspoon garlic powder

1 teaspoon onion powder

DIPPING SAUCE

½ cup mayonnaise

¼ cup plain, unsweetened soy milk *(not vanilla)*

1 teaspoon lemon juice

1 teaspoon onion powder

1 teaspoon garlic powder

1 teaspoon dried chives

½ teaspoon dried dill

½ teaspoon dried parsley

¼ teaspoon fine sea salt

¼ teaspoon ground black pepper

Prepare the chicken lollipops: In a medium bowl, whisk together the hot sauce, oil, vinegar, black pepper, cayenne, salt, garlic powder, and onion powder. Place the lollipops into the sauce; toss to coat. Marinate for at least 15 minutes or longer; you can transfer to a gallon-sized ziplock bag and marinate for hours in the refrigerator.

Prepare the dipping sauce: In a medium bowl, mix together the mayonnaise, soy milk, lemon juice, onion powder, garlic powder, chives, dill, parsley, salt, and pepper. Store in refrigerator until ready to serve. You can make this sauce a day or two in advance; the longer it sits, the better, to allow the flavors to marry.

Preheat your grill or grill pan (medium-high heat). Place chicken, with some marinade still clinging, on grill rack or in grill pan; grill chicken until cooked through and golden brown on all sides, turning frequently, about 30 minutes. Discard remaining marinade. Transfer lollipops to plates; serve with dipping sauce.

Drummettes are technically part of a chicken wing and are traditionally used to make lollipops, but require way too much effort for me for the one bite of meat that you get, so I like to use chicken drumsticks. Lay a drumstick on your cutting board. Using a chef's knife, cut off the very bottom joint. Using a paring knife or even a steak knife, grab that end firmly and cut through the skin surrounding the bone. Once you have gone all around, use your knife to scrape the meat up from the bone; use small scissors to trim off any sinews that appear. Use your fingers to grab the meat and push the meat down to the other end to make a nice plump lollipop.

MOZZARELLA in *carrozza*

If French toast married grilled cheese, this Mozzarella in Carrozza, literally "mozzarella cheese in a carriage," would be their glorious Neapolitan offspring. Slices of cheese are sandwiched between two slices of bread, breaded, and fried to ooey-gooey perfection. Dunk into some warm marinara for a perfect dish. Remember this one on Chanukah, when we indulge in all things fried plus dishes made with cheese.

 YIELDS **8 SERVINGS**

½ cup Italian seasoned breadcrumbs

½ cup all-purpose flour

4 large eggs

¼ cup milk

2 tablespoons grated Parmesan cheese

½ teaspoon fine sea salt

16 slices soft white bread

8 ounces fresh, good quality Buffalo mozzarella *(1 ball), cut into 8 round slices*

canola oil, *for frying*

warm marinara sauce

Mix the breadcrumbs and flour in a shallow container. Set aside.

In another shallow container, whisk the eggs, milk, Parmesan, and salt. Set aside.

Place two bread slices on your cutting board. Roll slightly with a rolling pin. Select a glass or cookie cutter almost as large as the bread slices. Use it to cut rounds from the bread. Discard the crusts.

Place one slice of mozzarella in the center of one bread round and top with a second bread round. Make sure there is at least ½ inch or more border of bread. If not, use a smaller cookie cutter to make smaller rounds of cheese. Press the bread rounds together. Wet the tines of a fork and seal the edges of the bread together by pressing the fork firmly into the bread all the way around. Repeat this with the remaining bread to make 8 sandwiches. Wet the fork as needed to help seal the bread.

Fill a pot or deep skillet with 2-3 inches of canola oil; heat over medium-high heat until the oil reaches 355°F.

Dip one sandwich into the egg mixture and coat on both sides. Tap off the excess; transfer to the breadcrumb mixture. Pat the breadcrumbs into the sandwich, coating both sides. Carefully slide the breaded sandwiches, a few at a time, into the hot oil; fry on both sides, until golden brown. Watch the oil closely and adjust the heat to keep from burning. Repeat with the remaining sandwiches. Serve immediately with the marinara sauce.

SEED *crackers*

In 2014, I did a cooking show in Toronto at the home of interior designer Heather Brown. I remember Heather's awesome walk-in refrigerator and her graciousness. She was an incredible hostess who supplemented my show with a number of her own creations. One of them was these incredible healthy seed crackers. They are grain-free, gluten-free, vegan, and yummy! She served them with chummos; I have served them with both chummos and black bean dip for a visually gorgeous appetizer, but they are awesome on their own as well.

I traced the recipe to Andrew Childs, a blogger, cookbook author, and guru when it comes to the paleo diet and lifestyle. He was thrilled to share it. Visit his website if you want to know more about the paleo lifestyle: http://thepaleodiet.co.za.

A Silpat silicone baking mat works great here, but if you don't have one, a parchment-lined cookie sheet will do. Psyllium husk is fiber (colon cleanse) that is so healthy for your body; in this recipe it absorbs the water and holds the crackers together. I found it easily at Whole Foods and online.

 YIELDS **8 SERVINGS**

1 cup raw sunflower seeds,
not roasted or salted

1 cup sesame seeds

¾ cup raw pumpkin seeds,
not roasted or salted

⅓ cup flax seeds

2 tablespoons psyllium husks

1 teaspoon fine sea salt

just over 2 cups water

Preheat the oven to 320°F. Prepare 2 Silpat baking mats or line 2 jellyroll pans or baking sheets with parchment paper.

Mix the sunflower seeds, sesame seeds, pumpkin seeds, and flax seeds in a bowl. Add psyllium husks and salt; combine with seeds very well.

Add water, stirring to make sure everything is mixed together well and that there are no dry clumps of psyllium.

Spread the wet mixture in a thin layer into 2 (11 x 16-inch) rectangles on prepared pans. Use a small offset spatula to spread it evenly and very thinly, making sure there are no gaps.

Bake, rotating in the oven every 15 minutes, until the crackers are somewhat baked. Remove crackers from oven when they are firm to the touch but not crispy, about 1 hour. Turn the crackers over and return to the oven for additional 20 minutes, until crispy. Turn off the oven and leave pans in turned-off oven until cooled. If they are moist at all, the crackers will be soggy when cooled, so make sure they are crisp all the way through. Remove from oven; break into shards of various sizes.

CHICKEN *flautas*

Flautas come from the Spanish word for flute. These rolled tacos are pan-fried until crisp and they resemble their namesake. They are a great way to start a meal, as they are both kid-friendly and loved by adults. This Mexican treat heats things up with spice and cools things down with the avocado cream.

If you are counting calories, you can try this baked version using corn tortillas. Cool the filling completely. Preheat the oven to 425°F. Coat 2 large jellyroll pans with cooking spray. Roll tortilla around filling; secure closed with toothpick as per the recipe. Set on prepared baking sheet. Repeat with remaining tortillas and filling mixture. Bake 6-10 minutes, or until tortillas are browned and crisp.

 YIELDS **12 FLAUTAS (6 SERVINGS)**

4 plump chicken thighs, *with skin and bone*

4 teaspoons taco seasoning, *divided*

1 tablespoon canola oil, *plus more for searing*

1 onion, *peeled, cut into ¼-inch dice*

¼ teaspoon cayenne

⅓ cup canned black beans, *rinsed and drained*

2 plum tomatoes, *seeded, cut into ⅛-inch dice*

¼ cup packed fresh cilantro leaves

12 small *(5-6-inch)* **flour tortillas**

2 ripe Haas avocados, *peeled and pitted*

¼ cup mayonnaise

2 teaspoons fresh lemon juice

additional fresh cilantro leaves, *chopped, for garnish*

Preheat the oven to 350°F.

Place the chicken thighs onto a small baking pan. Rub ½ teaspoon taco seasoning into each thigh, coating all the surfaces. Roast, uncovered, for 40 minutes. When cool enough to handle, discard the skin and bones. Coarsely chop the chicken. Set aside.

In a medium skillet, heat 1 tablespoon canola oil. Add the onion; sauté until shiny, 4-5 minutes; do not allow it to brown. Sprinkle in remaining 2 teaspoons taco seasoning, cayenne, and beans. Add the chicken; cook for 3 minutes. Remove the pan from the heat. Stir in the tomatoes and cilantro.

Place ¼ cup of the chicken filling into the center of each tortilla. Roll each tortilla tightly around the filling, securing each flauta with 1-2 toothpicks.

Heat 1 inch canola oil in an 8-quart pot. Using tongs, hold a flauta in the hot oil until firm, then release; cook until golden brown, about 2 minutes. Remove to a paper towel-lined plate. Discard the toothpicks. Repeat with remaining flautas.

In a food processor fitted with the metal "S" blade, pulse the avocado, mayonnaise, and lemon juice until smooth.

Serve 2 flautas per plate, topped with avocado cream and garnished with chopped cilantro.

spicy pickled **CARROTS**

Right near the Machane Yehuda market is a culinary treat called Khachapuria Restaurant. It was opened by Tango Sharvit, a Georgian Jew who left his job as an electrician to open an authentic Georgian bakery, serving the food he grew up on. His khachapuri, a yeast dough pastry, stuffed with grated Georgian cheese, butter, and poached egg, inspired a recipe that you will see later in the book (page 152). However, if that wasn't gift enough to my cooking repertoire, while I was waiting for my khachapuri to bake (each one is baked to order), they gave me a small serving of pickled carrots, which I devoured. My version is a bit spicier, but what a great crisp treat with which to start a meal! I like to keep these around as a healthy snack when I crave a crunch.

 YIELDS **6 SERVINGS**

4 **carrots,** *peeled, cut on the diagonal into ¼-inch slices*

1 **cup apple cider vinegar**

⅔ **cup water**

¼ **cup** *plus* **2 teaspoons sugar**

2½ **tablespoons mustard seeds**

1 **tablespoon dill seeds**

2 **dried bay leaves**

5 **sprigs fresh dill**

1 **clove fresh garlic,** *sliced*

Place the carrots into a 1-quart container or jar. Heat the vinegar, water, sugar, mustard seeds, dill seeds, and bay leaves in a small pot, stirring to dissolve the sugar; do not allow it to boil. Remove from heat; cool.

Pour the vinegar mixture over the carrots. Add the dill and garlic. Chill, covered, in the refrigerator at least overnight. The carrots will keep in this container for up to 3 weeks.

tuna SEVICHE tostados

The gorgeous Mexican coastline yields an abundance of fish, which yields an abundant number of ways to prepare it! Seviche "cooks" or pickles the fish with the acidity from the lime juice.

The freshness of the fish is vital. If you had tuna in mind for your menu but the snapper or grouper is fresher, swap out the fish. Store the fish on ice packs in your fridge until ready to use. I find it very helpful to have my fishmonger cut the fish for me. His intensely sharp blades glide through the fish like butter and make preparation of this dish a breeze.

Bring out a pitcher of margaritas and you have a fabulous no-cook new way to start your meal.

 YIELDS **6-8 SERVINGS**

1 pound very fresh raw tuna *or* **red snapper,** *skin removed, cut into ½ inch cubes; see note*

½ small red onion, *peeled, cut into ¼ inch dice*

1¼ cups fresh lime juice *(from about 10 limes)*

3 tablespoons extra-virgin olive oil, *divided*

1 firm beefsteak tomato, *seeded, cut into ½-inch dice*

½ English hothouse cucumber, *not peeled, seeded, cut into ½-inch dice*

½ small jalapeño, *finely minced*

2 tablespoons finely chopped fresh cilantro leaves

¼ teaspoon fine sea salt

¼ teaspoon freshly ground black pepper

1 ripe avocado, *peeled, pitted, cut into ½-inch dice*

good quality tortilla chips

Place the cubed fish and onion into a nonreactive glass or ceramic container just large enough to hold it. Pour in lime juice and 1 tablespoon olive oil; stir. Cover with plastic wrap; refrigerate for 30 minutes.

Meanwhile, in a medium bowl, mix the tomato, cucumber, jalapeño, cilantro, salt, pepper, and remaining 2 tablespoons oil. Toss together to blend flavors.

When the fish is ready, gently squeeze the fish and onion a handful at a time to drain off the lime juice; add fish and onion to the bowl, discarding the lime juice. Stir. The dish can be held at this point for up to 2 hours, covered, in the refrigerator. When ready to serve, add in the avocado. Serve napoleon-style layered on the tortilla chips.

Jewish ghetto, Venice, Italy

Corn fields, American Midwest

Lemons, Sorrento, Italy

Market day, Forte dei Marmi, Italy

Mexican avocados

Beresheet Spa, Mitzpe Ramon, Israel

Soups

RANCHERO *soup*

When teaching a class on Passover cooking at the Ritz Carlton in Cancun one year, I wanted to create a Southwestern soup that did not contain beans. This keeper, with its egg-drop soup effect, is so simple and is brightened with a pop of chilies, lime juice, and silky avocado.

 OR Ⓜ   YIELDS **8 SERVINGS**

1 tablespoon vegetable oil

1 onion, *peeled, cut into ¼-inch dice*

4 cloves fresh garlic, *finely chopped*

1 *(28-ounce)* **can diced tomatoes** *or* **whole peeled tomatoes,** *with their liquid*

4 cups chicken stock *or* **vegetable stock**

2 large eggs

½ jalapeño, *minced*

1 avocado, *peeled, pitted, cut into tiny cubes*

2 scallions, *green part only, thinly sliced on the diagonal*

¼ cup loosely packed cilantro leaves, *roughly chopped*

juice of ½ lime

additional limes, *cut into wedges, for garnish*

In a large soup pot, heat the oil over medium heat. Add the onion; cook until translucent, 5-6 minutes; do not allow it to brown. If it begins to brown, lower the heat. Add the garlic; cook for additional 3-4 minutes, until garlic is shiny.

Add the tomatoes with their liquid. If they are whole, use your hand to squeeze and burst them. Add the stock. Simmer, uncovered, over low heat, for 30 minutes.

In a small bowl, whisk the eggs. Whisk the soup and while whisking, slowly drizzle in the eggs, whisking all the time. Simmer for 4 minutes. Ladle into bowls.

In a small bowl, stir together the jalapeño, avocado, scallions, cilantro, and lime juice. Top each bowl with a spoonful of this garnish. Serve a lime wedge with each bowl.

PISTOU *soup*

Every single book that I used to prepare for teaching in Provence, France referenced pistou soup. Versions of this rustic soup abound in France, as it so beautifully reflects the fresh flavors of the area. I picked and chose my favorite elements for the recipe below.

If making this soup in advance, hold the pasta and canned beans until ready to serve. If making it for a dairy meal, sprinkle Parmesan over the pesto in each bowl. Serve with crusty bread or croutons.

 OR Ⓜ **YIELDS 6-8 SERVINGS**

2 cups *(2 ounces)* **firmly packed fresh basil leaves**

4 cloves fresh garlic, *ends trimmed, each cut in half*

¼ teaspoon kosher salt, *plus more as needed*

⅛ teaspoon white pepper, *plus more as needed*

½ cup extra-virgin olive oil

½ cup tubetti pasta, *or other shape the size of small beans*

1 tablespoon canola oil

½ red onion, *cut into ¼-inch dice*

1 carrot, *peeled, cut into ¼-inch dice*

20 green beans, *ends trimmed, cut into ¼-inch pieces*

1 yellow squash, *not peeled, cut into ¼-inch dice*

1 zucchini, *not peeled, cut into ¼-inch dice*

1 quart chicken *or* **vegetable stock**

1 *(14-ounce)* **can small white beans,** *rinsed and drained*

1 cup canned diced tomatoes

salt, *as needed*

pepper, *as needed*

Place the basil into the bowl of a food processor fitted with the metal "S" blade. Add the garlic, salt, and pepper. Purée. With the machine running, very slowly drizzle the olive oil down the feed tube until a pesto forms. Set aside.

Cook the pasta in a large pot of salted, rapidly boiling water according to the package instructions, until al dente. Drain; set aside.

Meanwhile, heat the canola oil in a large pot over medium heat. Add the red onion; cook until almost caramelized. Do not allow to burn; turn down the heat if needed. Add the carrot; sauté for 2 minutes. Add the green beans, squash, and zucchini; sauté for 2 minutes more. Add the stock; bring to a boil, then simmer for 10 minutes, until the vegetables are soft. Add the drained pasta, white beans, and tomatoes. Simmer for 5 minutes. Adjust salt and pepper as needed.

Ladle soup into each bowl. Swirl in a spoonful of the pesto.

beresheet spa CORN *soup*

The Beresheet Spa is one of my favorite spots in Israel. I work it into my tour itineraries every year and even made it a stop on my own family's personal tour this past summer for my son's bar mitzvah. It is built into the breathtaking edge of cliffs that slope into the Ramon Crater — an extraordinary natural phenomenon unparalleled in the world.

I had to force myself to come in from the exceptional views and surroundings but was rewarded with food at the Rosemary Restaurant that was absolutely divine. This soup was one of our group's favorites. Chef Michael Eshel was kind enough to show me how it was made. The recipe is a snap to make. The straining of the soup is a chore but essential to the creamy result.

YIELDS 8-10 SERVINGS

2 tablespoons canola oil

1 **small onion,** *peeled, cut into ½-inch pieces*

2 **stalks celery,** *cut into 2-inch chunks*

2 **cloves fresh garlic,** *roughly chopped*

1 **teaspoon ground turmeric**

2 **teaspoons salt**

½ **teaspoon ground white pepper**

¼ **teaspoon ground ginger**

2 **tablespoons sugar**

1 **tablespoon honey**

2 **pounds frozen corn kernels**

2 **potatoes** *(Idaho or Eastern are fine), peeled, cut into chunks*

slivered almonds

In an 8-quart soup pot, heat the canola oil. Add the onion, celery, garlic, and turmeric. Cook over medium heat until the vegetables are shiny, 5-6 minutes. Add the salt, white pepper, ginger, sugar, honey, corn, and potatoes. Cover with water by an inch or two. Bring to a boil; turn down to a simmer and cook, uncovered, for 40 minutes.

Transfer in batches to a blender. Purée in the blender, then pass soup through a chinois or fine mesh strainer. Discard the corn pulp. If the soup is still too thick, thin by whisking in hot water. Ladle into bowls; serve with a small handful of slivered almonds in each bowl.

TUSCAN BEAN and *farro soup*

The first European cooking class that I taught was in 2012, working for Eric Goldberg and Naomi Boutique Tours. No team is more indulgent of their guests than Eric's and no place is more indulgent of spectacular, magical fine food than Tuscany, Italy. My favorite memories of that trip include teaching about knives on a moving bus, scouring the markets of Forte dei Marmi, and bike riding around the glorious walled city of Lucca. Each day, after the group returned to the hotel, I returned to the kitchen to work with Gianluca Pardini of the International Academy of Italian Cuisine. He shared this recipe, which is an heirloom of Lucca itself. One whiff of this soup and I am transported back to that enchanted place.

Although the base of this soup is the borlotti bean paste that is made from cooking and processing the beans, canned cranberry or pinto beans will do in a pinch. This soup is meant to be served thick, almost like porridge, but thin it with additional stock if that is more to your taste.

 OR **M** YIELDS **6-8 SERVINGS**

1 cup dried borlotti beans *or* **cranberry beans,** *soaked 8 hours or overnight, with at least 2 inches of water to cover*

1 clove fresh garlic, *peeled*

10 fresh sage leaves, *divided*

1 fresh bay leaf

2 ribs celery, *plus* **3-4 leaves**

1 carrot, *peeled and quartered*

1 red onion, *peeled and halved*

leaves from 1 sprig rosemary

leaves from 1 stem fresh thyme

3 tablespoons extra-virgin olive oil, *divided*

2 tablespoons tomato paste

1 clove garlic, *minced*

3-4 cups chicken *or* **vegetable stock**

1 teaspoon salt

pepper, *to taste*

1 cup semi-pearled farro

extra-virgin olive oil, *to garnish*

red wine vinegar, *to garnish*

Place the beans with their water into a medium pot. Add additional water to cover the beans by at least 3 inches. Bring to a boil. Add the garlic, 6 sage leaves, and the bay leaf. Simmer for 45 minutes, until the beans are somewhat soft; they will finish cooking as the soup cooks.

Meanwhile, in the bowl of a food processor fitted with the metal "S" blade, finely chop the celery, celery leaves, carrot, onion, rosemary, thyme, remaining 4 sage leaves, and 1 tablespoon olive oil to make a "soffrito."

Heat remaining 2 tablespoons olive oil in a medium soup pot over medium heat. Add the soffrito; cook for 8-10 minutes until the vegetables are soft but not brown. Add the tomato paste and minced garlic; cook for 30 seconds, stirring with wooden spoon. Add this mixture to the pot of beans; continue cooking over low heat until beans are soft, about 40 minutes (longer if the beans were old). Remove and discard the bay leaf. Stir in 1½ cups water.

Using a blender, immersion blender, or food mill with medium-fine disc, purée the soup. The food mill is best in that it catches the bean skins so they can be discarded, but all of the methods work. If the soup is too thick for a blender, add in some warm water to get the blades moving. Place the puréed ingredients back into the soup pot; add 3 cups stock. Season with salt and pepper. Bring to a simmer. Add more liquid if necessary; it must have enough liquid to cover the farro, allowing it to cook. Add the farro; simmer, covered, for 25-30 minutes, stirring occasionally, until the farro is al dente and the soup is thick.

Ladle into bowls. Serve with a drizzle of olive oil and ¼ teaspoon red wine vinegar in each bowl.

If you did not soak the beans overnight, do a quick-soak: Place beans in a 4- to 5-quart pot; cover with cold water by 2 inches. Bring to a boil, uncovered; then boil 2 minutes. Remove from heat and let stand, covered, 1 hour.

CHEDDAR *ale* soup

The state of Wisconsin is known for its love affair with cheese. My daughter Kate, who studied that state for her fifth-grade state report, reminded me that it has more cows than people! And yes, people really wear cheesehead hats!

In 2009 I did a show for the Chabad in Milwaukee, Wisconsin. It was co-sponsored by The Spice House, which is one of the best-stocked small batch spice stores around. This soup would make a Wisconsinite proud and was developed with my Midwestern friends in mind.

You will definitely want a crusty loaf of bread with this delicious cheesy soup. It is best served fresh. Soups like this one, with heavy dairy ingredients, don't freeze well.

 YIELDS **10 SERVINGS**

2 tablespoons unsalted butter

2 tablespoons olive oil

1 medium Spanish onion, *peeled, cut into ½-inch pieces*

1 leek, *white and pale green parts only, cut into ¼-inch pieces*

4 cloves fresh garlic, *chopped*

1 stalk celery, *cut into ¼-inch pieces*

¼ cup all-purpose flour

1 (12-ounce) bottle lager beer, *such as Michelob*

2 cups vegetable stock, *plus additional for thinning if reheating*

1 cup lowfat milk

5 ounces block cream cheese, *at room temperature, cut into 5 pieces*

1 (8-ounce) bag shredded cheddar and mozzarella cheese blend

1 teaspoon Dijon mustard

¼ teaspoon Worcestershire sauce

fried onions, *French's or other brand, for garnish*

In a large pot over medium heat, melt the butter and heat the oil. Add the onion, leek, garlic, and celery. Cook until shiny and tender, 5-6 minutes; do not allow mixture to brown. If it begins to brown, lower the heat. Sprinkle in the flour to make a roux; it will be sticky.

Pour the lager beer around the vegetables, stirring with a wooden spoon or silicone spatula to pick up the floured vegetables that are stuck to the bottom of the pot.

Add the vegetable stock. Cook for 4-5 minutes to cook out the floury taste. Whisk in the milk. Turn the heat down to low. Whisk in the cream cheese and then the shredded cheese, a bit at a time, whisking the whole time. Never let the soup come to a boil.

Whisk in the mustard and Worcestershire sauce.

Ladle small portions (it is very rich) into bowls; garnish with fried onions. Serve piping hot.

FARRO, *chickpea,* and *white bean* soup

Beans and farro show up a few times in this section because they play such a big role in Italian cuisine. Having worked in various regions of Italy over many summers, I have fallen in love with both of these healthy ingredients and enjoy using them in recipes to serve my family.

 OR **M**   YIELDS **4-6 SERVINGS**

SOUP

2 tablespoons olive oil

2-3 small carrots, *peeled, cut into ¼-inch dice (¾ cup)*

3 medium shallots, *peeled, cut into ¼-inch dice (¾ cup)*

1 heaping tablespoon chopped fresh rosemary

1 *(15-ounce)* **can chickpeas,** *with their liquid*

1 *(15-ounce)* **can Great Northern** *or* **small white cannellini beans,** *with their liquid*

⅛ teaspoon ground white pepper

4 cups chicken *or* **vegetable stock**

½ cup *plus* **2 tablespoons semi-pearled farro**

PESTO

1 cup packed fresh basil leaves

2 cloves fresh garlic

2 tablespoons walnuts *or* **pine nuts**

¼ teaspoon fine sea salt

¼-½ cup extra-virgin olive oil, *plus additional for topping if needed*

¼ cup freshly grated Pecorino Romano *or* **Parmesan cheese,** *optional, for dairy meals*

Heat the oil in an 8-10-quart soup pot over medium heat. Add the carrots and shallots; sauté until shiny, 3-4 minutes; do not allow the shallots to brown. Add the rosemary, chickpeas with their liquid, white beans with their liquid, and white pepper. Cook for 2 minutes. Add the stock. Cook for 1 minute to heat the stock a bit. Add the farro; cook for 18 minutes.

Meanwhile, prepare the pesto: In the bowl of a food processor fitted with the metal "S" blade, process the basil, garlic, walnuts, and salt with on-off pulses until coarsely chopped. With the machine running, pour ¼ cup olive oil through the feed tube. Drizzle in more as needed to obtain desired consistency. Transfer to a container. Add the cheese, if using, for a dairy meal. If not using right away, or if freezing extra for future use, add enough olive oil to form an air-tight layer on top to protect the pesto from exposure to air. Set aside.

Using an immersion blender, blend half the soup with a few on-off pulses, leaving half of the soup not blended. Alternatively, transfer half the soup to a full-sized blender. Purée. Pour back into the pot. Warm through.

Ladle into bowls; swirl a teaspoon of pesto into each bowl. If made ahead, farro expands; you may need additional stock to thin soup to the desired consistency.

lemon CHICKEN SOUP
with orzo

Lemons grow in abundance all along the spectacular terraced gardens on the Amalfi coastline. Amalfi lemons possess a unique sweetness that results from a combination of the volcanic soil from Mt. Vesuvius, perfect Mediterranean temperatures, and just the right amount of rain.

   After working on the Amalfi Coast and in Sorrento in the summer of 2013, the iconic Amalfi lemons were my muse in the kitchen. I dreamed up this lemony chicken soup, which is perfect for a summer Shabbos dinner. If making this soup in advance, store the cooked orzo in a separate container, bring to room temperature, and add just before serving.

 YIELDS **6-8 SERVINGS**

2 tablespoons olive oil

½ **onion, peeled,** *cut into ¼-inch dice*

1 **carrot, peeled,** *cut into ¼-inch dice*

2 **dried bay leaves**

½ **teaspoon dried oregano**

¼ **teaspoon dried rosemary**

⅛ **teaspoon dried basil**

2 **chicken thighs,** *with bone and skin*

zest of 1 lemon

juice of 2 lemons

6 **cups chicken stock,** *low-sodium if possible*

½ **cup white wine**

1 **cup orzo**

2 **cups baby spinach leaves**

2 **tablespoons chopped fresh parsley leaves**

Heat the oil in a soup pot over medium heat. Add the onion and carrot. Sauté until shiny and translucent, 5-6 minutes, stirring occasionally. Add the bay leaves, oregano, rosemary, and basil. Cook for 2 minutes, until the spices are aromatic. Add the chicken, skin-side down; sear until the skin is nicely browned, 5-6 minutes. Don't move the chicken around while searing. Turn the chicken over; add the lemon zest, lemon juice, stock, and wine. Lower the heat; simmer, covered, for 45 minutes.

Meanwhile, cook the orzo in a pot of salted, rapidly boiling water according to the package instructions, for 1 minute less than recommended for al dente results. Drain, rinse in cold water, and drain again. Set aside.

Using tongs, remove and discard the bay leaves. Remove the chicken to a cutting board. Remove and discard the skin. Using two forks, remove the chicken from the bones; shred the chicken and return it to the pot. Add the spinach and parsley; cook until the spinach is wilted, 3-4 minutes.

Place scant ½ cup of the prepared orzo into each bowl. Ladle the soup over the orzo.

spicy LAMB MEATBALL soup

After returning from leading a culinary tour in Israel, lamb and lentils were on my mind, as were the bags of assorted spices that I had bought at the shuk. Succulent lamb meatballs in a flavorful, filling lentil soup were the result of my experimentation in the kitchen. This dish is a Middle Eastern flavor explosion in your mouth.

 YIELDS **8-10 SERVINGS**

2 tablespoons olive oil

1 yellow squash, *not peeled, cut into 1-inch chunks*

1 medium onion, *peeled, cut into 1-inch chunks*

1 large carrot, *peeled, cut into 1-inch chunks*

1 stalk celery, *ends trimmed, cut into 1-inch chunks*

4 cloves fresh garlic, *each cut in half*

1 teaspoon dried oregano

¼ teaspoon cumin

tiny pinch red pepper flakes

⅔ cup yellow lentils *or* **yellow split peas,** *divided*

8 cups chicken stock, *divided*

½ cup unflavored breadcrumbs

½ teaspoon fennel seeds

½ teaspoon ground black pepper

½ teaspoon paprika

¼ teaspoon cayenne pepper

¼ teaspoon smoked paprika

¼ teaspoon garlic powder

1 pound ground lamb

fresh chopped parsley, *for garnish*

Heat the olive oil in a soup pot over medium heat. Add the squash, onion, carrot, celery, garlic, oregano, cumin, and red pepper flakes. Cook until shiny and translucent, 5-6 minutes; do not allow any of the vegetables to brown. Add ⅓ cup lentils and 4 cups chicken stock. Reduce heat; simmer for 20 minutes or until vegetables are soft.

Meanwhile, prepare the meatballs: In a small bowl, mix the breadcrumbs, fennel seeds, black pepper, paprika, cayenne, smoked paprika, and garlic powder. Place the ground lamb into a mixing bowl; sprinkle on the spice mixture. Knead meat to distribute spices but don't overmix or the meatballs will be rubbery. Roll into 45 small meatballs.

When the vegetables have softened, use an immersion blender to purée the soup until smooth. Tilt the pot away from you to avoid splashing. This can also be done in a blender; return the soup to the pot after puréeing.

Add the remaining 4 cups chicken stock. Bring to a simmer. Add the meatballs and remaining ⅓ cup lentils. Cook, covered for 20 minutes.

Serve hot. Garnish with parsley.

SWEET POTATO *chestnut* **soup**

In studying for my trip to Northern Italy, I kept reading over and over how large parts of northern Italy are covered with "castagneti" (chestnut woods). For centuries chestnuts were the main source of food for the winter as the chestnuts were dried, made into polentas, flour, cakes, pastas, etc. Many of these dishes are still popular today. What I did not realize is that Italy, unlike America, is truly a seasonal country. When something is out of season, there is just no finding it. Summer is not chestnut season, so to my disappointment, nothing that I learned from the chefs there included chestnuts. I kept asking, they kept saying no. When I got home, I had such a craving for chestnuts that I worked on many recipes using the pouches of prepared chestnuts that are so readily available here. This soup was one of my favorite ways to use them.

 OR M YIELDS 10-12 SERVINGS

2 pounds *(4-5 medium)* **sweet potatoes**

1 tablespoon extra-virgin olive oil

2 leeks, *root ends trimmed, white and pale green part only, chopped*

2 stalks celery, *sliced*

leaves from 2 sprigs fresh dill, *to make 2 packed tablespoons*

leaves from 1 sprig fresh parsley, *to make 1 packed tablespoon*

½ teaspoon dried sage

⅛ cup brandy *or* **dry sherry**

2 *(3.5-ounce)* **bags chestnuts,** *roasted, shelled, ready-to-eat, divided*

6 cups chicken *or* **vegetable stock**

Preheat the oven to 350°F. Cover a baking pan with foil.

Roast the sweet potatoes on prepared pan, uncovered, for 1 hour, or until soft. Set aside until they are cool enough to handle. Peel the potatoes; discard skin.

Heat the oil in a large pot over medium heat. Add the leek and celery. Sauté until shiny, 4-5 minutes; do not allow to brown. Add the dill, parsley, and sage. Sauté for 2 minutes. Add the brandy; cook for 2 minutes. Add the sweet potatoes and half of the chestnuts to the pot. Pour in the stock. Bring to a boil. Turn down to a simmer; cook, covered, for 40 minutes.

Roughly chop or slice the remaining chestnuts to use as garnish. Set aside.

Transfer soup in batches to a blender or use an immersion blender right in the pot to purée the soup until smooth.

Ladle into bowls or mugs. Garnish with chestnuts.

shoyu tamago RAMEN soup

Once the noodles come out of the packaging, true Asian Ramen has almost no relationship to the "poor college kid on a budget" ramen or the junk that camp kids seem to crave. It is a hot, trendy food at the moment and this version is awesome. This is a fantastic all-in-one-bowl meal for a weeknight.

These gorgeous soy sauce eggs are often found in Japanese bento boxes as a snack or as part of lunch. I think they're best as a soft, runny addition to steaming ramen noodle soup, as in this recipe, but make extras for a salty snack all by themselves; they stay fresh for a week in the fridge.

 YIELDS **6 SERVINGS**

SOY SAUCE EGGS

3 cloves fresh garlic, *peeled, roughly chopped*

1 inch fresh ginger, *with skin, thinly sliced*

1 cup water

¾ cup soy sauce, *low sodium if possible*

½ cup mirin

⅛ teaspoon five-spice powder

6 large eggs *(older eggs are easier to peel)*

RAMEN SOUP

1 quart good-quality chicken soup *or stock*

½ teaspoon finely minced fresh ginger, *peeled*

2 cloves fresh garlic, *minced*

2 teaspoons soy sauce

½ pound London broil *(about half of a medium shoulder London broil)*

2 tablespoons canola oil

freshly ground black pepper

2 heads baby bok choy, *root ends trimmed, thinly sliced*

2 packs ramen noodles, *seasoning packets discarded*

Prepare the soy sauce eggs: Place the garlic, ginger, water, soy sauce, mirin, and five-spice powder into a small pot. Bring to a boil over medium heat; turn down to a simmer and cook on low for 8 minutes. Transfer to a 1-quart container; cool completely.

Set up a large bowl of water with 2 cups of ice in it. Fill a medium pot halfway with water. Bring to a gentle simmer. Carefully lower the eggs into the water; a spider or slotted spoon works well here. Simmer for 6½ minutes. During the first 2 minutes, gently stir the water with the handle of a wooden spoon to make a whirlpool to swirl the eggs in. This will center the yolks; be careful not to break the eggs. Using a slotted spoon, transfer the eggs to the ice water. Once cool, carefully peel the eggs. Tapping the fatter end of the egg on the side of the pot and then rolling it to crack the shell will make peeling easier.

Place the whole peeled eggs into the soy sauce mixture. Allow to marinate 6-8 hours in the refrigerator.

Prepare the ramen soup: When ready to complete the dish, remove the soy sauce eggs from the refrigerator so they can come to room temperature. Pour the chicken soup into a medium pot; bring to a simmer over medium heat. Add the ginger and garlic; simmer for 1 minute. Stir in the soy sauce. Turn off the heat. Set aside.

Cut the London broil in half lengthwise. Heat the canola oil in a medium skillet. Season the meat with pepper. Brown the meat, 2-3 minutes on each of the 4 sides, 8 minutes in total. Remove to cutting board to rest. After 10 minutes, slice as thinly as possible.

Return the soup to a simmer. Add the bok choy and ramen noodles. Cook for 3 minutes, stirring and pulling the noodles to separate them.

Using tongs, transfer the noodles to bowls. Cover with stock, distributing the bok choy among the bowls. Add the sliced steak. Halve each egg lengthwise, adding one egg to each bowl.

moroccan HARIRA

Traditional harira is sometimes served thickened with flour or with thin vermicelli noodles. I like it as is with a lighter stock. If you want the thicker result, mix 1 cup water with 1 cup flour and whisk it into the soup as it finishes cooking. If you want the noodles, add 2 ounces broken vermicelli noodles during the last few minutes of cooking and serve when the pasta is soft.

If you find chopping really tedious, you can use the food processor for the onions, carrots, celery, cilantro, and parsley.

 YIELDS **8 SERVINGS**

1 tablespoon canola oil

1 pound lamb *or* beef cubes

2-3 beef marrow bones

1 teaspoon turmeric

½ teaspoon ground ginger

½ teaspoon ground coriander

½ teaspoon cumin

½ teaspoon black pepper

½ teaspoon salt

½ cinnamon stick

2 onions, *peeled, finely chopped*

2 carrots, *peeled, finely chopped*

2 stalks celery with leaves, *finely chopped*

⅓ cup firmly packed cilantro leaves, *finely chopped*

¼ cup firmly packed parsley leaves, *finely chopped*

¾ cup green *or* brown lentils

1 (15-ounce) can chickpeas, *with their liquid*

1 (28-ounce) can diced tomatoes, *with their liquid*

7 cups chicken stock *or* water

½ lemon

chopped parsley *and* cilantro, *for garnish*

Heat the oil in a large pot over medium heat. Add the meat cubes and the bones. Brown the meat and the bones, turning with tongs as needed. Add the turmeric, ginger, coriander, cumin, pepper, salt, and cinnamon stick. Stir well to coat the meat.

Add the onions, carrots, celery, cilantro, parsley, lentils, chickpeas with their liquid, tomatoes with their liquid, and stock. Stir well. Bring to a boil. Reduce to a simmer; cook, covered, for 2 hours.

Squeeze the juice of the half lemon into the pot. Stir. If you used water in lieu of chicken stock, taste and season with salt as needed.

Ladle into bowls, discard cinnamon stick, and sprinkle with parsley and cilantro.

Lake Garda, Italy

The Salad Trail, Israel

Cranberry bogs, Massachusetts

Naot Goat Cheese Farm
Negev, Israel

Coast of Haifa, Israel

Arena di Verona, Italy

Salads

CARROT SALAD
with *honey dressing*

"Carottes râpées," or grated carrot salad, is a French classic. It is served at almost every bistro, market, and café. This one comes to us courtesy of the International Hotel chefs in Provence, France.

 YIELDS **6 SERVINGS**

SALAD

4 cups *(1 pound)* **shredded carrots**

handful chopped walnuts

chopped fresh parsley leaves, *for garnish*

DRESSING

⅓ cup honey

3 tablespoons lemon juice

2 tablespoons red wine vinegar

⅓ cup extra-virgin olive oil

1½ teaspoons minced fresh peeled ginger

½ teaspoon fine sea salt

¼ teaspoon freshly ground black pepper

Place carrots into a large bowl.

Prepare the dressing: Place the honey, lemon juice, and vinegar into a bowl. Whisking the whole time, drizzle in olive oil until a thick emulsion forms. Whisk in the ginger. Season with salt and pepper.

Toss dressing with carrots. Add walnuts; garnish with parsley.

provençal WHEATBERRY salad

The markets of Provence, France are legendary. Like a giant traveling carnival, vans, trucks, and pushcarts unload their wares throughout the town, filling the air with fun, music, life, and fragrance. You can walk for miles just gathering the most perfect, fresh ingredients to take home and create food with — recipes not required. I try to channel this exhilarating feeling as spring and summer approach in this country, and farmers markets pop up in town after town. I can never pass one up. I love interacting with the farmers and hearing passion when they describe their offerings. This salad, great cold or warm, is an ode to markets all over the world.

YIELDS **8-10 SERVINGS**

1 cup hard red winter *or* soft white wheatberries

3 cups water

½ teaspoon fine sea salt

25 green beans, *ends snipped, quartered, to make 1 cup*

½ pint grape tomatoes

5-6 radishes, *ends trimmed, thinly sliced, then cut into thin strips*

15 Kalamata olives, *pitted, chopped*

3 tablespoons extra-virgin olive oil

2 tablespoons Dijon mustard

½ teaspoon fine sea salt

¼ teaspoon black pepper

4 mint leaves, *sliced into thin ribbons*

4 basil leaves, *sliced into thin ribbons*

handful sliced *or* slivered almonds

zest of ¼ lemon

Place the wheatberries, water, and salt into a small pot. Bring to a boil; reduce heat to a simmer. Cook for 35 minutes, until the wheatberries are soft; drain off any excess water. Transfer wheatberries to a large bowl.

Steam or microwave the green beans until bright green, 3 minutes steamed or 1½ minutes in the microwave with 1 tablespoon water. Drain; add to the bowl. Add tomatoes, radishes, and olives.

Drizzle with olive oil, mustard, salt, and pepper. Mix well. Sprinkle with the mint and basil.

Transfer to serving bowl. Sprinkle on the almonds; zest the lemon over the top.

lara restaurant **BEET** salad

Lara is a quaint restaurant in Jerusalem. Michelin-starred Italian chef Lior Chaftzadi creates an Israeli menu with worldwide influences, all set in a romantic, artistic room with an open kitchen. On my 2015 Foodie Tour of Israel, our group ate our first dinner together there. The food was creative and overflowing, which made it hard to pick a favorite, but this raw beet salad was deemed a smash. Off I ran to the kitchen, where they happily recreated it for me so I could share it here with you.

 YIELDS **6-8 SERVINGS**

4 **large red beets,** *peeled, cut into thin slices, then into julienne matchsticks*

2 **cloves fresh garlic,** *minced*

3 **scallions,** *thinly sliced on diagonal*

¼ **cup loosely packed, fresh cilantro leaves,** *chopped*

3 **tablespoons soy sauce**

4 **tablespoons silan** *(date syrup)*

4 **teaspoons lemon juice**

1 **tablespoon extra-virgin olive oil**

2 **teaspoons roasted sesame oil**

pinch of salt

⅛ **teaspoon freshly ground black pepper**

small handful honey-roasted peanuts *or* **caramelized hazelnuts** *(egozei Luz), chopped, for garnish*

In a large mixing bowl, toss the beets, garlic, scallions, and cilantro.

Prepare the dressing: In a small bowl, whisk together the soy sauce, silan, lemon juice, olive oil, and sesame oil. Season with a small pinch of salt and pepper.

Drizzle dressing onto beets to taste; you may have extra dressing. Toss well. Taste; add more salt and pepper as desired.

Garnish with chopped nuts.

LUMINA *market salad*

Chef Meir Adoni has it all: smarts, charm, and an incredibly creative head in the kitchen. After winning the world's attention with his restaurants in Tel Aviv, he turned his attention to the kosher world and gifted it with Blue Sky and Lumina restaurants in the Carlton Hotel in Tel Aviv. He is a true innovator and it shows even in a salad as simple as the one below. This market salad blends textures, flavors, and visual appeal, while each ingredient sings on its own.

 YIELDS **6-8 SERVINGS**

3 **Persian cucumbers,** *not peeled, quartered lengthwise*

1 **kohlrabi,** *peeled, cut into small pieces*

2 **red radishes,** *not peeled, halved and sliced*

¼ **small red onion,** *cut into ¼-inch dice*

½ **small fennel,** *cut into paper-thin slices; use a handheld mandolin if possible*

6-8 **cherry tomatoes,** *quartered*

large handful pea shoots *or* **mâche lettuce**

2 **scallions,** *sliced*

parsley leaves from 3 stems, *chopped*

2 **tablespoons fresh lemon juice**

6 **tablespoons extra-virgin olive oil**

½ **teaspoon fine sea salt**

¼ **teaspoon freshly ground black pepper**

In a large bowl, toss the cucumbers, kohlrabi, radishes, onion, fennel, tomatoes, pea shoots, scallions, and parsley.

In a small bowl, whisk together lemon juice, olive oil, salt, and pepper. Dress salad to taste.

carmel spa
POMEGRANATE *almond salad*

My first Foodie Tour of Israel with the Jewish Journey included the Carmel Forest Spa in Haifa. All the luxuriating and relaxing works up an appetite, and the spa lived up to its reputation for sensational food. The salads were among the favorites of the offerings. What I loved about this one was the explosion of bitter, tangy, sweet, spicy, and peppery. It made it irresistible.

 YIELDS **6 SERVINGS**

DRESSING

1 tablespoon pomegranate molasses

1 tablespoon honey

3 tablespoons fresh lemon juice

1 teaspoon dried basil leaves

1 teaspoon Dijon mustard

½ teaspoon garlic powder

½ teaspoon ground dried ginger

¼ teaspoon red pepper flakes

5 tablespoons extra-virgin olive oil

SALAD

3 ounces red leaf lettuce, *torn into bite-sized pieces*

2 ounces arugula leaves

½ cup whole raw almonds, *not roasted or salted*

⅛ cup pomegranate seeds

4 fresh mint leaves, *roughly torn*

leaves from 3 stems fresh cilantro, *roughly chopped*

crumbled feta cheese, *to taste*

Prepare the dressing: In a small bowl, whisk together pomegranate molasses, honey, lemon juice, basil, mustard, garlic powder, ginger, and red pepper flakes. Whisk quickly as you slowly drizzle in the oil. It is best to make the dressing a day in advance to allow the flavors to mellow and meld. If the dressing becomes too thick, whisk in one more tablespoon of olive oil.

Place the lettuce and arugula into a large bowl. Top with almonds, pomegranate seeds, mint, cilantro, and feta cheese.

Drizzle dressing over salad to taste.

lentil and TUNA salad

Lentils, dubbed the "poor man's meat," are a low-cost source of protein. This delicious recipe is a typical Tuscan picnic dish. It can be made in advance, is healthy, and travels well. It is a perfect addition to a shalosh seudos table or a great summer Shabbos appetizer. Seek out the Italian or French Puy lentils; they make a huge difference in taste and texture. They are nothing like the mushy soup lentils you may be familiar with. They are hearty, intensely flavored, and keep their shape perfectly.

 YIELDS 6-8 SERVINGS

1 carrot, *peeled*

1 rib celery

½ white onion, peeled

1½ cups French Puy lentils *or* **lenticchie di Castelluccio**

6 whole black peppercorns

2 teaspoons red wine vinegar

1 *(15-ounce)* **can diced tomatoes**

coarse sea salt *or* **kosher salt**

1 *(200-gram)* **can tuna,** *preferably Rio Mare or other Italian tuna packed in olive oil; don't drain*

leaves from 4 sprigs fresh thyme

⅛ teaspoon cayenne pepper

2 tablespoons extra-virgin olive oil

2 teaspoons balsamic vinegar

sprigs of fresh thyme, *for garnish*

Maldon *or* **other flaky salt,** *for garnish*

Fill a medium pot halfway with cold water. Add carrot, celery, onion, lentils, peppercorns, and red wine vinegar. Bring to a boil.

Place the tomatoes into a strainer to drain; discard liquid. Set aside.

Check the lentils after about 20 minutes, although they may need closer to 30 minutes. Not all lentils cook in the same amount of time, so you will need to taste one. They should be slightly al dente, not mushy and falling apart but not hard. When the lentils are almost done, add 1 teaspoon coarse salt. Stir.

Drain the lentils, rinsing in cold water to stop the cooking. Pick out and discard the carrot, celery, and onion. Place lentils into a large bowl.

Add drained tomatoes and tuna with its oil. Add the thyme, cayenne, olive oil, and vinegar. Stir. Season to taste with more coarse salt, at least ½ teaspoon.

Drizzle with additional olive oil; garnish with a sprig of fresh thyme and a small pinch of Maldon salt.

STEAK SALAD
with sumac red onions

Sumac bushes, which grow in the Middle East, produce deep reddish/purplish berries. The berries are ground to make a spice that adds a tart lemony flavor to recipes. Sumac is a great way to add an acidic balance with a gorgeous pop of color to a dish. Dust it on chicken, chummos, in olive oil, any dish that uses feta … the list goes on and on. You will see it again in this book in the Meze Burger recipe. Sumac is often an ingredient in the popular za'atar spice blend.

 YIELDS **6-8 SERVINGS**

SALAD

1 **red onion,** *peeled, halved, cut into ¼-inch slices*

1 **teaspoon sumac**

1½ **pounds minute steak fillet, filet split, skirt steak,** *or* **London broil**

1 **teaspoon fish-free Worcestershire sauce**

7 **tablespoons extra-virgin olive oil,** *divided*

salt

pepper

5 **ounces spring mix** *or* **baby greens**

10 **cherry tomatoes, mix of yellow and red,** *each halved*

DRESSING

2 **tablespoons pomegranate syrup** *or* **pomegranate molasses**

1 **tablespoon red wine vinegar**

1 **tablespoon Country Dijon mustard**

¼ **teaspoon fine sea salt**

¼ **teaspoon freshly ground black pepper**

Place the onion slices into a medium bowl. Toss with the sumac to coat all the slices. Set aside.

Place the steak into a glass container or baking dish just large enough to hold it. Massage in the Worcestershire sauce and 3 tablespoons olive oil to coat both sides.

Heat 1 tablespoon olive oil in a large grill pan or skillet over medium-high heat. Season the steak with salt and pepper. Add onion to the pan; cook until tender, about 4 minutes. Push onions to the side; add the steak, searing 3-6 minutes per side or until medium rare. Thicker London broil will take much longer and the onions may need to be removed from the pan if they start to burn. Transfer steak to a cutting board; allow to rest for 10 minutes before slicing.

Meanwhile, prepare the dressing: In a medium bowl whisk the pomegranate syrup, vinegar, mustard, salt and pepper. Whisk in the remaining 3 tablespoons extra-virgin olive oil.

Arrange the greens and tomatoes on a platter. Drizzle with just enough dressing to coat lightly. Slice the steak across the grain; arrange on and in the salad. Toss the onions on top. Drizzle with additional dressing.

BOK CHOY *chicken salad*

I am always looking for new chicken salads that can be served warm or cold. This one, with its crunch and Asian flavors, is a winner.

 YIELDS **6-8 SERVINGS**

2 tablespoons low-sodium soy sauce

1 tablespoon mirin

1 tablespoon dark brown sugar

1 teaspoon cornstarch

4 cloves fresh garlic, *minced*

¼ teaspoon dried ground ginger

⅛ teaspoon ground white pepper

1½ pounds boneless, skinless chicken breasts, *cut into 1-inch cubes*

2 tablespoons canola oil

2 heads baby bok choy, *chopped*

6 cremini mushrooms, *sliced*

½ cup unsalted cashews

¼ cup water *mixed with* 1 teaspoon soy sauce

½ lemon

3 ounces baby spinach leaves

2 teaspoons roasted *or* toasted sesame oil

1 teaspoon seasoned rice vinegar

1 ripe mango, *peeled, pitted, cut into ¼-inch dice*

In a medium bowl, whisk the soy sauce, mirin, brown sugar, cornstarch, garlic, ginger, and white pepper. Add the chicken cubes; marinate for 10 minutes.

Heat the oil in a large (14-inch) skillet over medium-high heat until very hot but not smoking. Add the chicken with all the marinade. Sauté for 4 minutes; the chicken will not be cooked through. Use tongs to turn each piece of chicken. Add the bok choy, mushrooms, and cashews. Sauté for 3-4 minutes until the bok choy is shiny and almost wilted. Add the water/soy sauce mixture to the pan. Use a wooden spoon to scrape the browned bits from the bottom. Squeeze the half lemon over the pan. Sauté 1 minute longer; remove from heat.

Spread the spinach onto a platter or place into a serving bowl. Drizzle with the sesame oil and rice vinegar. Toss to coat. Top with the cooked bok choy/chicken mixture; garnish with mango. Serve warm or at room temperature.

EDAMAME, *corn, pepper* salad

While this recipe was only inspired by my travels around the corner, it was too good and too easy not to include. My friend Michelle Plotsker gave me this recipe. It is great at a barbecue, brunch, shalosh seudos meal, or for last-minute company, since I always have most of the ingredients on hand in my freezer and pantry. What is travel-inspired is my addition of corn nuts, which are not really nuts but fried kernels of corn. I discovered them in an airport on a delayed flight to Pittsburgh and knew I had to include them in a recipe. They are a perfect salty, crunchy addition to this or any salad.

 YIELDS **10 SERVINGS**

SALAD

2 red bell peppers, *seeded, cut into ¼-inch dice*

1 *(15-ounce)* **can** *or* **2 cups frozen white shoepeg corn,** *drained, defrosted in microwave if frozen*

1 *(15-ounce)* **can** *or* **2 cups frozen yellow corn,** *drained, defrosted in microwave if frozen*

1 *(12-ounce)* **bag shelled edamame,** *defrosted in microwave if frozen*

large handful corn nuts *(toasted corn snack),* *for garnish*

DRESSING

1 packet Good Seasons Italian dressing mix

¼ cup balsamic vinegar

3 tablespoons water

½ cup extra-virgin olive oil

Place the peppers, corn, and edamame into a large bowl.

Prepare the dressing: Empty the seasoning packet into a jar or cruet. Add the vinegar, water, and oil. Shake vigorously to combine.

Pour dressing over the vegetables. Marinate for 15 minutes.

Garnish with corn nuts.

KALE squash *caesar salad*

Homemade croutons are best; the stale taste of packaged ones can sometimes ruin a salad. Cut the crusts from a day-old baguette. Cut the bread into cubes. Toss with olive oil, salt, and 3-4 minced fresh garlic cloves. Bake on a parchment-lined cookie sheet at 350°F until toasted and dried, 20-25 minutes. You can store the croutons in a ziplock bag for 2 weeks.

 D OR **P** **YIELDS 8-10 SERVINGS**

SALAD

1½ pounds *(1 medium)* **butternut squash,** *peeled, seeded, cut into 1-inch cubes; can use pre-cut squash cubes*

½ teaspoon fine sea salt

¼ teaspoon freshly ground black pepper

3 cloves fresh garlic, *minced*

1 tablespoon canola oil

1 bunch *(6-7 stems)* **curly kale**

1 small head Romaine lettuce; *can use one Romaine heart*

½ cup hazelnuts

½ small red onion, *peeled, thinly sliced*

1-2 handfuls croutons; *see note above*

shaved Parmesan cheese, *for dairy meal*

DRESSING

1 cup full-fat mayonnaise

4 teaspoons lemon juice

2 teaspoons Worcestershire sauce

1 teaspoon garlic powder

1 teaspoon onion powder

½ teaspoon freshly ground black pepper

Preheat the oven to 400°F. Line a cookie sheet or jellyroll pan with parchment paper.

Place the squash on prepared pan. Sprinkle with salt and pepper. Mix with the garlic. Drizzle with oil. Toss to coat well. Spread in an even layer. Roast for 20-25 minutes. Set aside. Lower the oven temperature to 375°F.

Strip the leaves from the kale stems; discard stems. Place the leaves into a bowl of cold water. Soak and rinse the leaves. Tear into bite-sized pieces; place into a large bowl.

Finely chop the Romaine; add it to the bowl.

Place the hazelnuts into a small ovenproof pot. Place, uncovered, into the oven; toast for 15 minutes. The skins will crack. Transfer to a kitchen towel or paper towels; roll the nuts around to remove most of the skin. Cut each nut in half. Add to the salad. Sprinkle in the red onion. Add the roasted squash.

Prepare the dressing: In a small bowl, whisk together the mayonnaise, lemon juice, Worcestershire sauce, garlic powder, onion powder, and pepper.

Dress the salad, coating the lettuce well. Transfer to serving bowl. Top with croutons and cheese, if using.

root vegetable **APPLE** salad

Kohlrabi is a knobby purple or green vegetable with a taste and texture somewhere between cabbage and broccoli stems. They were all over Machane Yehuda market when I was there in February, and I knew I wanted to include them somewhere in this book. Cut off the leaves and use a vegetable peeler to remove the thick green skin.

Celery root is another ugly duckling at the produce department but once you trim off both ends and cut away or peel off the thick skin, you will love the distinctive flavor — think: combination of celery and parsley. I turn to it again and again for cooking in creamy soups, roasting as a side dish, or crisp and raw in salads like this one.

This recipe was inspired by Ali Mafucci, of the Inspiralized website, which is a great website for recipes that use a Spiralizer, or spiral slicer. The apples work great on that machine and add a fun texture to the salad. If prepping in advance, soak the peeled vegetables and apple in water with some lemon juice added. This acidulated water will keep everything from turning brown.

 OR **P**   YIELDS **6-8 SERVINGS**

SALAD

1 small kohlrabi, *peeled and trimmed*

½ celery root (celeriac), *peeled and trimmed*

1 small turnip, *peeled and trimmed*

1 Granny Smith apple, *not peeled*

2 handfuls baby arugula leaves

handful sweetened dried cranberries

handful chopped walnuts

¼ cup crumbled goat cheese, *optional, for dairy meals*

DRESSING

¼ cup honey

2 tablespoons red wine vinegar

2 tablespoons Country Dijon mustard

6 tablespoons extra-virgin olive oil

¼ teaspoon fine sea salt

⅛ teaspoon freshly ground black pepper

Cut the kohlrabi and celery root into thin matchsticks. Grate the turnip on the large holes of a box grater. Cut the apple into small chunks or use a spiral slicer to make it into "noodles." Place into a large mixing bowl.

Toss with the arugula. Sprinkle in cranberries, walnuts, and cheese, if using.

Prepare the dressing: In a medium bowl, whisk together the honey, vinegar, mustard, oil, salt, and pepper.

Dress the salad to taste.

chedva's warm
FRENCH POTATO SALAD

My friend Chedva Hubsher is one of a kind: thoughtful, sensitive, erudite, and wacky in the best possible way. She served me this potato salad one Shabbos lunch and I was wowed. The purple/blue spuds are show-stoppers and the taste is wonderful. She offered me the recipe for inclusion in the book. I asked if it was original, as otherwise I wouldn't be able to use it. Her response was that it started out as Ina Garten's, a personal favorite author of mine, but for sure was original because it turned out that it was stuck to another recipe in Chedva's file, so unbeknownst to her, she had combined the two, ended up loving it even more, and then added her own touches. Just hilarious.

Leftovers can be served at room temperature the next day. For a dairy twist, add crumbled goat cheese to the potatoes while they are warm so that the cheese can melt in.

 YIELDS **6-8 SERVINGS**

¼ cup kosher salt

2 pounds assorted baby potatoes, *combination of purple or blue, pink, and white ones*

8 ounces haricots verts, *each cut into thirds*

¼ cup white wine, *such as Sauvignon blanc*

2 shallots, *peeled, very finely minced*

¼ cup Dijon mustard

¼ cup lemon juice

¼ cup extra-virgin olive oil

6 fresh basil leaves, *chopped*

⅓ cup fresh dill, *chopped*

⅓ cup parsley leaves, *chopped*

1 teaspoon chopped fresh rosemary

1 teaspoon fleur de sel, purple sea salt, *or other finishing salt*

Fill an 8-quart pot ¾-full with water. Add the kosher salt. Bring to a boil. Add the whole potatoes; boil for 20 minutes, until fork-tender.

Meanwhile, place the haricots verts into a microwave-safe bowl with 1 tablespoon water; cook for 1 minute. Drain. Transfer to a large mixing bowl.

Drain the potatoes. Cool until safe to touch, 5-6 minutes. Cut each into halves or thirds, depending on size. Add to the bowl. Drizzle with the wine. Add the shallots.

In a small bowl, mix together mustard, lemon juice, and olive oil. Pour over the potatoes; stir to coat. Toss in the basil, dill, parsley, and rosemary; mix well.

Garnish with finishing salt. Serve warm.

curly SWEET POTATO salad

Big crunch, big curl, huge fun ... this salad is irresistible.

I have done shows in both South Carolina and North Carolina. Both had lovely and warm Jewish communities. I was fascinated to learn that since 1971, North Carolina has ranked as the number-one sweet potato-producing state in the U.S. Its hot, moist climate and rich, fertile soil are ideal for cultivating sweet potatoes, averaging nearly 50% of the U.S. supply. This recipe is in honor of all the great people who showed me their Southern hospitality on those visits.

 YIELDS **4-6 SERVINGS**

2 medium sweet potatoes, *peeled*

canola oil

fine sea salt

⅓ cup mayonnaise

3 tablespoons balsamic vinegar

2 tablespoons maple syrup

3 ounces fresh baby spinach leaves

2 ounces mesclun lettuce *or* spring mix

handful sweetened dried cranberries

handful chopped pecans

Cut off both ends of each sweet potato to make flat surfaces. Attach to a spiral slicer; make thin, spaghetti-like noodles from the sweet potatoes. Crank right over a cookie sheet to catch the potatoes as they fall. Discard the core.

Heat 2 inches canola oil in a large skillet until hot but not smoking. Fry the sweet potatoes until brown; do not allow them to burn. Transfer immediately to a paper towel-lined plate. Salt them while they are warm.

Prepare the dressing: In a small bowl, whisk together the mayonnaise, vinegar, and maple syrup. Set aside.

Place the spinach and mesclun into a medium bowl. Add the cranberries and pecans. Drizzle with balsamic dressing to taste. Divide among plates or place on a platter, making sure to distribute the cranberries and pecans evenly. Top with the curly sweet potatoes.

STADIUM *salad*

Over the years, I have been invited to give shows in almost all of the 50 states. Every time I took a flight to a place that had a Major League stadium, I would make a pit stop to the stadium to buy a souvenir hat and to take a picture of myself in front of the stadium. I would quickly email the picture to my baseball-loving young son, Eli, so he would know where I was. In honor of those memories, I came up with this salad, a salute to the baseball experience. Pretzels, hot dogs, peanuts ... and caps off to my friend Linda Gruenbaum for the yummy dressing.

 YIELDS **6 SERVINGS**

SALAD

3 large handfuls mini pretzel twists

2 tablespoons spicy brown mustard

1 tablespoon favorite barbecue sauce

2 large chicken cutlets, *cut into 1-inch cubes*

¼ cup canola oil, *divided*

3 hot dogs, *cut into ¼-inch thick slices*

3 ounces lettuce of choice

handful cherry tomatoes, *roughly chopped*

½ English hothouse cucumber, *seeded, cut into ¼-inch dice*

½ cup honey roasted peanuts

1 cup pretzel crisps, *broken*

DRESSING

½ cup canola oil

¼ cup sugar

2 tablespoons white vinegar

2 teaspoons soy sauce

2 teaspoons yellow mustard

1 clove crushed garlic, *can use frozen*

Place the pretzel twists into the bowl of a food processor fitted with the metal "S" blade. Process until they resemble breadcrumbs. Transfer to shallow bowl or container.

In a second shallow bowl or container, combine the spicy brown mustard with the barbecue sauce. Coat the chicken cubes in the mustard mixture, then bread in the pretzel crumbs. Set aside.

Heat 2 tablespoons canola oil in a large skillet. Add the hot dog slices; sauté until golden brown, caramelized, and slightly puffed. Use tongs to flip slices to caramelize both sides. Remove to a bowl; do not wipe out the pan. Add 2 more tablespoons canola oil to the pan. Add the coated chicken cubes; sauté until golden brown on all sides and chicken is cooked through, 3-4 minutes total. You may need a little more oil if preparing the chicken in batches.

Meanwhile, prepare the dressing: In a 1-pint container, whisk or shake together the ½ cup canola oil, sugar, vinegar, soy sauce, yellow mustard, and garlic until smooth and emulsified.

Place the lettuce into a large bowl. Add the tomatoes and cucumbers. Top with the pretzel-crusted chicken, hot dogs, and peanuts. Add dressing to taste. Garnish with broken pretzel crisps.

Milan, Italy

Lavender fields
Provence, France

Spices
Machane Yehuda,
Jerusalem, Israel

Drying pasta, Italy

Tuscan streetscape, Italy

Amalfi coastline, Italy

Poultry

ROSEMARY LAVENDER *chicken*

Summertime is the season to seek out the spectacle of stunning purple lavender surrounding the Luberon villages in Provence, France. The color, texture, and scent of lavender are at the heart of this area's fame. While there, I visited the Lavender Museum to learn about the healing properties of lavender, experience the lotions, teas, medicinal properties, and — most important to me — the beauty of cooking with culinary lavender. The gorgeous flecks of purple in this dish and its role in the herby French spice blend Herbs du Provence cause this dish to shine. Serve this chicken over an herbed rice pilaf.

 YIELDS **4-6 SERVINGS**

1 **chicken,** *cut into eighths*

1 **tablespoon canola oil**

¼ **teaspoon kosher salt**

½ **cup wildflower** *or* **clover honey**

4 **teaspoons Herbs du Provence;** *select one that is heavy on the lavender. I like Morton and Basset brand*

1 **teaspoon dried rosemary,** *chopped*

¼ **teaspoon cayenne**

¼ **cup red wine vinegar**

fresh rosemary sprigs *or* **other fresh herbs,** *for garnish*

Preheat the oven to 400°F.

Place the chicken into an oven-to-table casserole dish. Massage the canola oil into the chicken; sprinkle with salt.

In a small bowl, combine the honey, Herbs du Provence, rosemary, cayenne, and vinegar. Set aside.

Bake the chicken for 35 minutes, uncovered. Then, baste the chicken every 10 minutes with the honey-lavender mixture until cooked through and nicely browned. Total cooking time should be about 1 hour.

Garnish with fresh rosemary sprigs or other fresh herbs.

ROASTED CHICKEN *with cauliflower* and brussels sprouts

A perfect fall meal all in one pot. One year, my Israel Foodie Tour dined in a hidden gem of Israel, Bachatzer shel Ora. We enjoyed a unique Yemenite meal in a beautiful orchard. Yementite-born Ora and Polish-born Reuven are charming hosts. The marinade on this chicken is based on a favorite dish that we ate there.

 YIELDS **4-6 SERVINGS**

CHICKEN

3 **tablespoons olive oil**

12 **ounces** (about ½ large head) **cauliflower florets**

8 **ounces Brussels sprouts,** *root ends trimmed, each halved*

1 **chicken,** *cut into eighths, with bone and skin*

MARINADE

¼ **cup yellow mustard**

2 **tablespoons honey**

2 **teaspoons paprika**

2 **teaspoons za'atar, dried herb** *or* **spice blend**

1 **teaspoon hawaij spice blend**

½ **teaspoon black pepper**

½ **teaspoon salt**

2 **tablespoons canola oil**

2 **tablespoons water**

Preheat the oven to 450°F. Place a small pan of water in the oven while it preheats; this will make the oven atmosphere moist.

Line a jellyroll pan or large roasting pan with foil. Pour in the olive oil. Toss the cauliflower and Brussels sprouts in the oil, coating well; spread vegetables in an even layer in the pan.

Prepare the marinade: Combine the mustard, honey, paprika, za'atar, hawaij, pepper, salt, oil, and water. Mixture should be creamy.

Arrange the chicken in the pan in a single layer, skin-side up; do not overlap the pieces. Nestle the chicken parts between the cauliflower and sprouts, leaving some of the vegetables uncovered. Brush the marinade onto all sides of the chicken; add a nice thick layer of marinade on top.

Bake, uncovered, for 30 minutes. Then cover with foil; bake an additional 20-30 minutes, until the chicken is no longer pink inside. Transfer chicken and vegetables to serving platter.

amalfi SAGE chicken

Gorgeous crisp browned skin, incredible perfume of fresh herbs. This winner will surely become a favorite chicken dinner. It takes me right back to a kitchen that I worked in on the Amalfi Coast, where a team of chefs whipped this up for "family meal," the meal the staff eats. One whiff and I was desperate to become a member of the family.

 YIELDS **4-6 SERVINGS**

3 tablespoons olive oil

1 **chicken,** *with bone and skin, cut into eighths*

6 **whole garlic cloves,** *in their skin if possible*

fine sea salt

1 **small pepperoncini red chili** *or* **¼ teaspoon red chili flakes**

2 **large sprigs fresh rosemary**

6 **leaves fresh sage,** *roughly torn, plus additional for garnish*

3 **leaves fresh basil,** *torn*

1 *(750-ml)* **bottle dry white wine**

Heat the olive oil in a very large (14-inch) skillet over medium-high heat. Add the chicken, skin-side down, and the garlic. Sear the chicken until the skin is very crisp and brown. Be patient and don't move the pieces around too much. Wear long sleeves and be careful, as the oil may pop. Using tongs, turn each piece. Season with a sprinkle of salt. Break the chili in half and add it to the pan with the rosemary, sage, and basil.

Add white wine around the perimeter of the skillet to come halfway up on the chicken parts. Be aware that the wine may ignite; it will burn off in a few moments.

Simmer on medium-low, uncovered, for 30 minutes. Add more wine if it cooks out too quickly.

Transfer to a platter; garnish with the roasted garlic, pan juices, and the additional sage.

MUSTARD CAPER *chicken*

This recipe has Tuscan flair with its capers, lemon, and garlic. Stick a post-it note on the page and return to it again and again when looking for a memorable chicken dinner.

 YIELDS **4 SERVINGS**

1 **Idaho potato,** *peeled*

2 **whole lemons**

2 **teaspoons dried oregano**

2 **tablespoons spicy brown** *or* **natural stone ground mustard**

½ **teaspoon black pepper**

1 **chicken,** *cut into eighths*

3 **tablespoons canola oil**

4 **cloves fresh garlic,** *smashed with the side of a knife*

1 **onion,** *peeled, cut into 8 chunks*

12 **button mushrooms,** *quartered*

3 **tablespoons capers,** *in salt or brine, rinsed well*

¼ **cup lemon juice**

Preheat the oven to 375°F.

Cut the potato in half lengthwise. Then cut each half into ½-inch-thick half-moons. Place into a 9 x 13-inch casserole dish. Set aside.

Zest one of the lemons, placing the zest into a small bowl and reserving the lemon. Add oregano, mustard, and black pepper to the zest, stirring to combine. Using a spoon or small spatula, coat the skin side of the chicken with the mustard mixture.

Heat the oil in a large skillet over medium heat. Place the chicken, skin-side down, into the hot oil; sear, browning the mustard and the chicken skin. Transfer to the casserole dish, placing the chicken, skin-side up, on the layer of potatoes. Do this in batches if necessary.

To the skillet add the garlic, onion, and mushrooms. Cook for 1 minute. Thinly slice the zested lemon and add it to the skillet along with the capers. Squeeze the juice of the second lemon over the mushroom mixture; add the squeezed lemon to the chicken. Scrape up the browned bits from the skillet. Spoon the mixture over the chicken; drizzle with lemon juice.

Bake, uncovered, 1 hour 30 minutes. Serve hot.

Brined capers retain their acidic vinegar taste even after rinsing. Seek out salt capers for a more intense, and fresh caper flavor and better texture. Remember to rinse well. They can easily be found online.

EGGPLANT *chicken*

This rustic dish is sure to be a real crowd-pleaser. It is great over a bed of farro or angel hair pasta, to take it back to its Italian roots.

 YIELDS **4-6 SERVINGS**

8 chicken parts, *with bone and skin (thighs and breasts; no wings)*

½ teaspoon fine sea salt

½ teaspoon freshly ground black pepper

2 tablespoons canola oil

1 Italian eggplant, *not peeled*

1 onion, *peeled, cut into ½-inch dice*

4 cloves fresh garlic, *sliced*

2 cups canned diced tomatoes, *with their liquid*

½ teaspoon dried oregano

⅛ teaspoon cayenne pepper

½ navel orange

Preheat the oven to 375°F.

Season the chicken with salt and pepper. Heat the oil in a large skillet over medium heat. Add the chicken, skin-side down, to sear it and get some color on the skin. Do this in batches as needed. Transfer the chicken to a 9 x 13-inch oven-to-table casserole dish.

Meanwhile, cut the eggplant in half lengthwise; then cut each half lengthwise into 3 sticks. Cut each stick into chunks.

Once all the chicken is seared, add the eggplant chunks to the pan, allowing them to soak up the fat from the chicken. Stir the eggplant after it has browned on some of the surfaces. Add onion and garlic. Sauté for 2 minutes. Add the tomatoes with their liquid, oregano, and cayenne. Simmer for 3 minutes. Squeeze the juice from the half orange into the pan. Stir. Pour mixture over the chicken.

Bake, uncovered, for 1 hour 15 minutes. Serve hot.

firecracker TURKEY burger

Every part of this dish, from the pickled onions to the creamy cilantro honey mayo to the healthy turkey burger, is divine and an explosion of flavor and texture.

 YIELDS **4 SERVINGS**

PICKLED ONIONS

1 cup white vinegar

1 cup water

2 tablespoons kosher salt

1 tablespoon sugar

¼ teaspoon fennel seeds

2 dried bay leaves

1 red onion, *peeled, halved, thinly sliced*

CILANTRO HONEY MAYO

½ cup fresh cilantro leaves, *finely chopped (1 tablespoon)*

½ cup light mayonnaise

1 tablespoon honey

zest and juice of ½ lime

TURKEY BURGERS

1 pound ground turkey, *blend of dark and white meat*

1 tablespoon soy sauce

1 teaspoon kosher *or* coarse salt

1 teaspoon cumin

1 teaspoon garlic powder

½ teaspoon cayenne pepper

4 burger buns

Romaine lettuce

sriracha sauce

Prepare the pickled onions: In a small pot, over medium heat, heat the vinegar, water, salt, sugar, fennel seeds, and bay leaves. Stir to dissolve salt and sugar.

Place the onion slices into a 1-quart container. Separate the slices. Pour the vinegar mixture over the onions. Let stand until it cools to room temperature. Place in refrigerator until ready to use, up to 2 weeks ahead.

Prepare the cilantro honey mayo: In a small bowl, whisk the cilantro, mayonnaise, honey, lime zest, and lime juice. Set aside.

Prepare the burgers: In a medium bowl, with gloved hands that have been sprayed with nonstick cooking spray, combine the turkey with the soy sauce, salt, cumin, garlic powder, and cayenne. Mix well to distribute the spices. Form into 4 burgers.

Heat a grill pan over medium-high heat until very hot but not smoking. Spray with nonstick cooking spray. Cook the burgers 4 minutes per side until cooked through; do not overcook.

Spread the cilantro honey mayo on both sides of each bun. Top each with some Romaine leaves, a burger, and some of the pickled onions; drizzle with sriracha sauce.

chicken ADOBO

Although the name is Spanish, adobo is a cooking method from the Philippines. With its marinating sauce of vinegar, soy sauce, and garlic, adobo will win you over with its simple toss-together steps. The marinade does all the heavy lifting here. The chicken sits for a few hours or overnight, absorbing the flavors, while the hit of spices during the cooking finishes the dish with a flavor that will drive you wild.

 YIELDS **4-6 SERVINGS**

1 **chicken,** *spatchcocked or quartered*

½ **cup white vinegar**

½ **cup soy sauce**

2 **cloves fresh garlic,** *minced*

1 **tablespoon garlic powder**

1 **teaspoon onion powder**

½ **teaspoon ground black pepper**

½ **teaspoon ground coriander**

1 **medium onion,** *peeled, cut into chunks*

Place the chicken into a large, heavy-duty ziplock bag. Combine the vinegar, soy sauce, and minced garlic. Pour it into the bag; marinate the chicken for two hours or up to overnight in the refrigerator.

In a small bowl, combine the garlic powder, onion powder, pepper, and coriander.

Preheat the oven to 375°F.

Place the chicken into an oven-to-table dish that fits the chicken without overlapping or squishing it. Pour on the marinade. Sprinkle the spice blend over the chicken; pat it onto each part. Surround chicken with onion chunks.

Bake, uncovered, for 1 hour. Drizzle with pan juices.

TURKEY BREAST
with *hoisin tangerine glaze*

A turkey breast is so simple to work with, don't save it just for holiday meals. This sweet and sassy version is a winner. The glaze turns a plain old turkey breast into a show-stopper.

 YIELDS **6 SERVINGS**

1 *(3-4 pound)* **turkey breast with wing, bone, and skin**

3 tablespoons **Cajun spice mix**

3 tablespoons **orange marmalade**

2 tablespoons **hoisin sauce**

1 teaspoon **roasted** *or* **toasted sesame oil**

zest and juice of 1 tangerine *or* **clementine**

bunch fresh cilantro, *for garnish*

Preheat the oven to 350°F.

Place the turkey breast, wing up, in a roasting pan that it fits well.

Prepare the glaze: In a medium bowl, stir together the Cajun spice, marmalade, hoisin, sesame oil, zest, and juice of the tangerine. Mix until well blended.

Brush all the glaze over the turkey. Cover with foil that has been coated with nonstick cooking spray and tented so that it doesn't stick to the marinade. Roast, covered, for 30 minutes. Uncover; roast for an additional hour.

Transfer to a platter. Garnish the platter with fresh cilantro.

dried fruit & *quinoa* STUFFED CAPONS

For a two-year stretch, I did regular cooking shows at Pomegranate Supermarket — a "Disney World" for a food lover. My job was to incorporate their prepared sauces, dips, sides, cuts of meat, and salads into recipes. I spent many joyous hours roaming their aisles with my creative juices flowing, and the shows were always a blast. This is a version of a recipe I wrote for them. When we photographed it, my whole team took home copies of the recipe, my favorite acknowledgement that I have a winner. Perfect for a holiday table.

 YIELDS **6 SERVINGS**

1 cup quinoa

2 cups water

1½ teaspoons salt, *divided*

5 jumbo apricots

2 dried pitted prunes

⅓ cup Chinese pecans *or* glazed pecans

1 tablespoon silan *(date syrup)*

¼ teaspoon black pepper

6 boneless capons, *with skin*

½ cup good quality plum, blackberry, *or* fig jam

Chinese pecans *or* glazed pecans, *chopped, for garnish*

Preheat the oven to 375°F.

Coat an oven-to-table casserole dish with nonstick cooking spray. Set aside.

If the quinoa package does not state that it is pre-rinsed, rinse the quinoa by placing it into a medium bowl, covering with water, swishing it around, and then draining it in a strainer. This will wash away any naturally occurring bitterness. Place the drained quinoa into a medium pot. Add water and 1 teaspoon salt. Bring to a boil. Lower to a simmer; allow the quinoa to bubble and cook for 15 minutes until all the liquid is absorbed. The outer germ layer will separate and the grains will look shiny. Add more water if needed during the cooking process. Set aside.

Place the apricots, prunes, and pecans into the bowl of a food processor fitted with the metal "S" blade. Pulse only until nuts are chopped; don't run the machine or they will become a paste. You should see the colors and pieces of apricot and prune. Add this mixture to the cooked quinoa along with the silan, remaining ½ teaspoon salt, and pepper.

Open a capon and place it skin-side down on a cutting board. Add some of the quinoa mixture down the length of the capon, leaving a border clear. Roll the capon to enclose the quinoa. Place the rolled capon, cut-side down, into the prepared dish. Repeat with the remaining capons; you may have extra quinoa.

Microwave the jam for 30 seconds to make a thin glaze. Brush onto capons. Roast capons, uncovered, for 30 minutes, or until no longer pink inside. Turn on the broiler; broil for 5-6 minutes, until nicely colored. Garnish with chopped pecans.

udon **CHICKEN NOODLE** *bowl*

Slide over, stir-fry — udon is the new bowl of comfort food. This Japanese-style chicken dish is the perfect meal on a chilly or rainy day. The thick wheat-based noodles are chewy and very filling; try them in soups as well.

 YIELDS **6 SERVINGS**

1 pound boneless, skinless chicken breasts, *each cut lengthwise into thin strips*

1½ tablespoons cornstarch

1 tablespoon water

⅓ cup hoisin sauce

3 tablespoons soy sauce

3 tablespoons sugar

8 ounces mung bean sprouts

10 scallions, *bright green part only, each cut into 4-5 thin, long strips using tip of knife*

1 *(8.8-ounce)* **package udon noodles** *or* **thin fettuccini**

2 tablespoons canola oil

1 inch fresh ginger, *peeled, cut into 8-10 very thin slices*

1 medium onion, *peeled, halved, and cut into ¼-inch slices*

Place the chicken into a medium bowl. Mix with the cornstarch and water until chicken is coated. Set aside.

In a small bowl, combine the hoisin, soy sauce, and sugar. Set aside.

Bring a large pot of water to a boil. Add the bean sprouts and scallion strips. Blanch for 30 seconds. Using a spider or a strainer, remove from pot, reserving the water. Set aside.

Return water to a boil. Cook the udon noodles according to package instructions for 1 minute less than recommended for al dente results. Drain. Set aside.

Heat the oil in a large skillet over high heat. When the oil is hot but not smoking, add the chicken, ginger, and onion. Sauté for 7-8 minutes, until chicken is just cooked through. Add the noodles and sauce mixture. Stir to heat through. Add the bean sprouts and scallions, using tongs to toss.

Transfer to serving bowl.

slow roasted
HONEY-SPICED chicken

Nothing says Shabbos dinner to me like roast chicken. Slow-roasting it keeps the meat nice and moist. The mostly hands-off cooking time makes this version a joy.

 YIELDS **4-6 SERVINGS**

1 *(5-pound)* **whole chicken**

3 tablespoons olive oil, *divided*

20-24 small Yukon gold potatoes, *halved lengthwise*

pinch kosher *or* **coarse salt**

1 **lemon,** *cut lengthwise into quarters*

10-12 **whole garlic cloves,** *peeled*

2 tablespoons honey

SPICE RUB

2 tablespoons dark brown sugar

1 tablespoon kosher *or* coarse sea salt

1 tablespoon sweet paprika

1 tablespoon chili powder

1 tablespoon garlic powder

1 teaspoon freshly ground black pepper

Preheat the oven to 300°F. Select a rectangular or oval shaped, shallow roasting pan that is just slightly bigger than the chicken. Brush 1 tablespoon olive oil evenly over the bottom of the pan.

Arrange the potatoes tightly in the pan, cut-side down, forming a raft that will elevate the chicken out of its juices, allowing it to cook more evenly. Trim potatoes as needed to fit pan so that they are in a tight single layer without any wiggle room. Drizzle the potatoes with 1 tablespoon olive oil; lightly sprinkle with salt. Set pan into the sink.

Prepare the spice rub: In a small bowl, combine the brown sugar, salt, paprika, chili powder, garlic powder, and pepper. Use your fingertips to really blend evenly.

Place the lemon and garlic cloves into the cavity of the chicken. Cross the legs and tie with kitchen twine or silicone band.

Hold the chicken over the pan (lots of the spices will fall off), with the legs up to keep the lemons and garlic inside; rub the spice mixture all over the chicken, getting a nice thick coating on all parts. Place breast-side up onto the potatoes. Drizzle with remaining tablespoon olive oil. Drizzle the honey over the chicken, starting at the legs; it will drip toward the neck due to its angle.

Slow-roast, uncovered, for 2½-3 hours, slightly less for a smaller chicken. At the 2-hour mark, brush with the pan juices. Check temperature after 2½ hours. A thermometer inserted into the thickest part of the thigh, not touching bone, should read 165°F. Let chicken rest for 10 minutes before carving.

ISRAELI SPICED *chicken*

A walk through Machane Yehuda Market in Jerusalem is like a walk back in time to a spice-traders' world. The colors, the aromas, the good-natured shouting are all part of the sensory experience. While I eat a lot of foods on the spot, what I bring home are the spices. A few pinches of this and that and you have a dynamite dish that can transport you to the place we all love. In the United States, buy Pereg brand spices, if possible — I think they are the freshest.

  YIELDS **6 SERVINGS**

6 boneless, skinless chicken breasts *or* **thighs** *(pargiyot)*

3 tablespoons extra-virgin olive oil

1 tablespoon turmeric

1 teaspoon garlic powder

1 teaspoon dried oregano

1 teaspoon schwarma spice

½ teaspoon cumin

½ teaspoon salt

½ red onion, *peeled, sliced into ½-inch-thick slices*

Heat a grill pan until very hot.

While pan is heating, place the chicken into a bowl. Drizzle with olive oil; with gloved hands, rub into the chicken.

In a small bowl, combine the turmeric, garlic powder, oregano, schwarma spice, cumin, and salt.

Sprinkle cutlets with spice mixture; rub to coat well. Toss the red onion into the bowl with the chicken. Allow to stand for 10 minutes.

Grill the chicken with the onions, 7-8 minutes per side. Serve hot. This dish goes well with Israeli couscous or salad.

Itai's **FOUR-ONION** chicken

My 13-year-old son has a sweet and adorable friend named Itai Merlin. Itai had a rough break on the soccer field and had to take a "vacation" from sports over the summer. A great attitude and a smart mother led him to the kitchen, where he cooked up some awesome food. He took a serious stab at cooking and his results were impressive. With tremendous pride, he shared this recipe with me, and I am thrilled to share it with you. Add "chef" to the long list of possible futures for this kid.

 YIELDS **4-6 SERVINGS**

1 tablespoon extra-virgin olive oil, *plus additional to rub on chicken*

½ teaspoon yellow mustard seeds

1 onion, *peeled, halved, thinly sliced*

1 red onion, *peeled, halved, thinly sliced*

1 leek, *root trimmed, white and light green parts only, thinly sliced lengthwise into strands*

1 shallot, *peeled, halved, thinly sliced*

2 cloves fresh garlic, *thinly sliced*

1 chicken, *cut into eighths*

extra-virgin olive oil

1½ teaspoons ground yellow dried mustard

¾ teaspoon fine sea salt

¼ teaspoon freshly ground black pepper

½ cup white wine

½ cup brandy *or* sherry

3 tablespoons honey

Preheat the oven to 400°F.

Heat the oil in a large skillet. Add the mustard seeds and heat until they pop. Add the onion, red onion, leek, shallot, and garlic. Sauté over medium heat until wilted, 5-6 minutes. Transfer to a 9 x 13-inch casserole dish, spreading vegetables in a thin layer.

Arrange the chicken, skin-side up, in a single layer over the onions. Brush the chicken parts with olive oil. Combine dried mustard, salt, and pepper in a small bowl. Sprinkle on the chicken. Combine the white wine and the brandy. Pour over the dish to distribute evenly.

Microwave the honey for 20 seconds. Drizzle over the chicken parts.

Bake, uncovered, for 30 minutes. Baste with pan juices; bake for an additional 20 minutes until chicken is golden, flesh is no longer pink, and onions have cooked down. Baste with pan juices.

Serve the chicken with the onions piled on top.

Terra di Seta winery, Tuscany, Italy

Mexican cantina

Lake Como, Italy

Artisanal bread
Shuk HaCarmel,
Tel Aviv, Israel

Tortillas on grill, Mexico

Texas cattle

Meat

MEZE *burger*

I kicked off my 2015 Israel Foodie Tour with a cooking demonstration. In developing the burger for that show, I wanted to use as many Middle Eastern ingredients as possible, to whet the appetites of the participants for what they would experience in the upcoming days. The chickpeas in the burger, the crunch of the sumac onions, the creaminess of the techina, the hit of za'atar in the olive oil, the crisp grilled eggplant: this one rang every bell. You will LOVE it.

 YIELDS **4 BURGERS**

1 cup chickpeas *(may be canned)*

1 pound ground beef

2 teaspoons schwarma spice

1 medium eggplant

extra-virgin olive oil

1 teaspoon kosher salt

1 **onion,** *halved, thinly sliced*

1 tablespoon sumac

1 teaspoon za'atar

2 teaspoons techina

1 **small beefsteak tomato,** *thinly sliced*

1 **English or Persian cucumber,** *not peeled, cut into paper-thin slices*

6 **Kalamata olives,** *pitted and chopped*

4 burger buns

Place the chickpeas into a large bowl. Using a potato masher, mash the chickpeas. Add the ground beef and schwarma spice. Mix well to combine. Divide and shape into 4 burgers.

Slice the eggplant into 4 (½-inch-thick) slices, the same diameter as the burgers. Place into a bowl; drizzle with olive oil and kosher salt. Rub the oil in; allow to tenderize for a few minutes.

Place the onion slices into a small bowl. Toss with the sumac and 2 teaspoons olive oil. Set aside.

In a small bowl or ramekin, combine the za'atar with 1 tablespoon olive oil.

Coat a nonstick grill pan with nonstick cooking spray. Heat the pan until very hot but not smoking. Grill the eggplant, trying not to move it around so you get nice grill marks on both sides. Remove to a platter; set aside. Re-spray the pan; sear the burgers, 6-7 minutes per side.

Assemble the burgers: Spread ½ teaspoon techina on one side of the bun and spread a little of the za'atar mix on the other side. Place a burger on the bottom half of a bun. Top with eggplant slice, tomato, cucumber, sumac onions, and olives. Top with second half of bun. Repeat with remaining burgers and buns.

BEEF *pizzaiola*

Pizzaiola hails from Naples. It was invented to tenderize less-expensive cuts of beef. The meat is seared and then braised in pizza sauce until tender. It is easy to make and a way to get an authentic Italian dinner on the table in 15 minutes flat!

 YIELDS **6 SERVINGS**

olive oil

1½ pounds *(about 3)* **shoulder steak cutlets,** *pounded very thin by butcher into 4 x 11-inch rectangles, then each cut in half widthwise*

salt

black pepper

dried oregano

4 cloves fresh garlic, minced

2 cups chopped fresh cherry tomatoes; *can use assorted colors*

2 cups warm marinara sauce

chopped fresh parsley, *for garnish*

Heat 2 tablespoons olive oil in a very large skillet. When very hot but not smoking, add the steaks, searing 45 seconds per side; they will still be rare. You will need to do this in batches. Lay the steaks into a jellyroll pan, mostly in a single layer. Sprinkle with pinches of salt, pepper, and oregano.

Add another tablespoon of oil to the pan in which the steaks were cooked. Add the minced garlic; cook over medium heat until fragrant. Add the cherry tomatoes and marinara sauce. Tilt the pan that is holding the meat to allow any meat drippings to pour into the tomato sauce. Taste the sauce; season with salt, pepper, and oregano. Simmer for 5 minutes.

Place the steaks into the sauce. Cover the pan. Cook for 5 minutes. Uncover the pan and turn the steaks; cook for a final 4-5 minutes.

Garnish with a drizzle of olive oil and chopped parsley.

veal SCALLOPINI

Although the term "escalope" is French, meaning "thin slices of meat," Veal Scallopini originated in Italian cuisine. The mushrooms make this dish sing and I always prepare extra to use in other dishes such as rice, or to tuck into an omelet for the next day's meals. The meat cooks in minutes; make sure to stay alert so as to not allow it to overcook and toughen.

 YIELDS **4-6 SERVINGS**

extra-virgin olive oil

25 whole button mushrooms, *wiped clean*

white wine

3 tablespoons olive *or* canola oil

⅓ cup all-purpose flour

1 teaspoon salt

½ teaspoon freshly ground black pepper

1½ pounds good-quality thin veal scallopini *(less than ¼-inch thick)*

3 cloves fresh garlic, *minced*

2 tablespoons chopped flat-leaf parsley, *plus extra for garnish*

Pour a thin layer of extra-virgin olive oil to coat the bottom of a stock pot. Add whole button mushrooms; cook for 3 minutes over medium heat, stirring occasionally. Add white wine to come up halfway on the mushrooms. The amount will depend on the size of your pot. Cover the pot. Allow to simmer for 30 minutes; the mushrooms won't change color but they will become shiny and softer. Remove from heat. Remove the mushrooms, reserving the liquid. Allow to cool.

Heat a large heavy skillet (not nonstick) over high heat until hot. Add 3 tablespoons oil; heat until it shimmers.

In a shallow container, stir together flour, salt, and pepper. Pat veal dry with paper towels; dredge in the seasoned flour, tapping off excess.

Cook veal in 2-3 batches, turning once, until browned and just cooked through, 2-2½ minutes per batch. Transfer to a platter; keep warm. Do not wipe out the pan.

Reduce heat to low. Thinly slice the prepared mushrooms. Add the garlic to the pan; sauté for 2 minutes, until fragrant. Add the sliced mushrooms, reserved cooking liquid, and 2 tablespoons chopped parsley. Sauté for 3-4 minutes until warmed through, fragrant, and shiny.

Top each veal scallopini with mushrooms. Garnish with parsley.

LAMB SHANKS
with date gremolata

My inspiration for this fragrant dish is Moroccan Tagine. The layering of aromatics, spices, wine, and citrus are a kaleidoscope of textures and tastes. Dates and silan are the common themes that run through the dish and its bright pesto topping.

 YIELDS **4 SERVINGS**

LAMB SHANKS

4 lamb shanks *(4 pounds)*

⅛ teaspoon fine sea salt

¼ teaspoon black pepper

2 tablespoons canola oil

2 parsnips, *peeled, cut into 1-inch chunks*

1 carrot, *peeled, cut into 1-inch chunks*

1 onion, *peeled, cut into ½-inch chunks*

1½ cups peeled butternut squash cubes *(roughly 1-inch chunks)*

3 cloves fresh garlic, *sliced*

1 cinnamon stick

1 star anise

2 cups dry white wine, *such as Chardonnay or Sauvignon Blanc*

3 cups beef stock or **chicken stock**

3 tablespoons silan *(date syrup)*

1 cup orange juice

GREMOLATA

⅓ cup toasted pine nuts

¼ cup loosely packed parsley leaves

½ cup dried dates, *pitted, chopped*

zest from ½ orange

Preheat the oven to 350°F.

Season the lamb shanks with salt and pepper.

Heat the oil in a Dutch oven or heavy pot over medium heat. Add the shanks; brown them on all sides, using tongs to rotate them. Do this in batches as needed and remove to a baking sheet when browned.

Add parsnips, carrot, onion, squash, and garlic to the pot. Use a wooden spoon to scrape up the browned bits from the bottom of the pot. When the vegetables are shiny, after 5-6 minutes, add the cinnamon stick and star anise.

Add the wine and stock. Allow it to bubble; then cook until it reduces by half. Return the lamb to the pot. Drizzle the silan around the lamb. Simmer for 1 minute. Add the orange juice; the lamb does not need to be completely submerged. Reduce heat to medium-low. Cover the pot. Cook for 3 hours. Allow the meat to cool in the pot in its liquid.

Prepare the gremolata: Place the pine nuts, parsley, dates, and zest into the bowl of a food processor fitted with the metal "S" blade. Pulse to make a thick pesto.

Serve each lamb shank with a heavy sprinkle of gremolata.

ragu NAPOLITANO

Real Italian peasant food at its finest! Serve this hearty dish over rigatoni to catch the sauce, open a bottle of wine, unwrap some crusty bread, and gather some good people.

 YIELDS **8 SERVINGS**

1 tablespoon olive oil

2 carrots, *trimmed, not peeled, cut into ¼-inch dice*

2 stalks celery, *cut into ¼-inch dice*

1 onion, *peeled, cut into ¼-inch dice*

5 cloves fresh garlic, *finely chopped*

1 tablespoon dried oregano

1 teaspoon freshly ground black pepper

1 cup good-quality dry red wine

1 *(12-ounce)* **pack cured hot Italian sausages,** *such as Jack's*

2 lamb shanks *or* **osso bucco**

4 large marrow bones

3 *(28-ounce)* **cans crushed tomatoes**

56 ounces *(2 tomato cans)* **water**

1-2 pounds rigatoni, *cooked al dente according to package directions*

Heat the olive oil in a large pot over medium heat. Add the carrots, celery, onion, and garlic. "Sweat" the vegetables, 4-5 minutes, until shiny; do not brown. Add oregano and pepper. Cook for 2 minutes, stirring to release and toast the spice. Add the wine. Reduce heat to a simmer. Cook down for 5 minutes.

Add sausages, lamb shanks, and marrow bones. Top with the tomatoes and water. Bring to a boil, then turn the heat to low; simmer, uncovered, on the lowest heat. You should have nice, light bubbling, like 3-4 small volcanoes. Cook for 1 hour 15 minutes. Remove the sausages, lamb shanks, and marrow bones. Reserve to serve with sauce.

Add Braciole (see page 130), if desired. If not cooking Braciole, just continue to simmer the ragu for an additional hour. Turn off the heat; allow to cool for 45 minutes, uncovered. Serve the ragu over the rigatoni and the meats.

BRACIOLE

Braciole, pronounced "bra-zhool," is a dish that every Italian family makes as part of Sunday sup-per. It is found in almost every region in Italy, using all different types of meat. I learned this dish from a traditional Neapolitan, Chef Damian Sansonetti. In Naples they use beef and he recom-mended shoulder steaks as the best choice for a kosher cook. The thinly pounded beef (best left to the butcher to do) is stuffed, rolled, tied, browned, and then left to simmer for hours in the tradi-tional Sunday sauce. It is moist and loaded with flavor. I may not have been born into this tradition, but it is one I have happily adopted on occasion.

 YIELDS **4-6 SERVINGS**

1½ pounds *(about 3)* **shoulder steak cutlets,** *pounded very thin by butcher into 4 x 11 rectangles*

1 onion, *peeled and quartered*

8 cloves fresh garlic

6 fresh mint leaves

6 large basil leaves *(½ cup loosely packed)*

½ teaspoon red pepper flakes

1 teaspoon coarse *or* **kosher salt**

½ cup unflavored dry breadcrumbs

1 tablespoon canola oil

During the final 2 hours of the Ragu Napolitano cooking time (see page 128), prepare the braciole. If not making the ragu, warm about 3 quarts of jarred marinara sauce over low heat.

In the bowl of a food processor fitted with the metal "S" blade, pulse the onion, garlic, mint, basil, red pepper flakes, and salt. Pulse using on-and-off pulses, scraping down the sides often. You want small bits, not a paste. Place into a bowl. Blend in the breadcrumbs, a tablespoon at a time, to make a paste. Press into a thin layer on each steak, leaving a 1-inch border on all sides. Roll up each steak; tie with butcher's twine in 3 places on each roll to secure it.

Heat the canola oil in a skillet. Sear the rolls on all sides. Don't crowd the pan; do in batches if necessary.

Refer to the Ragu Napolitano recipe (page 128): After you have removed the sausage, lamb shanks, and marrow bones from the ragu, place the braciole into the pot. Cook for 1 hour; do not allow the sauce to boil. Then, allow the braciole to stand in the sauce, with the heat turned off, for 45 minutes. If not making the ragu, simmer the meat rolls in the marinara sauce.

When cooled, slice on the diagonal into pinwheels. Serve with ragu sauce.

pumpkin braised SHORT RIBS

If autumn had a celebrity dish, this would be it. These short ribs will be the reason your succah or Thanksgiving table is the place to be. The long, slow cooking time yields rich, succulent results.

If the ribs don't come tied, you can use kitchen twine or silicone bands. It's just for prettier presentation so that they don't fall off the bone.

 YIELDS **5-6 SERVINGS**

½ **cup all-purpose flour**

½ **teaspoon ground sage**

½ **teaspoon fine sea salt**

½ **teaspoon freshly ground black pepper**

6 pounds *(10-12 large ribs, each 4 x 2 inches)* **thick short ribs,** *each tied*

2 tablespoons canola oil

1 onion, *peeled, cut into ½-inch dice*

24 ounces *(2 [12-ounce] bottles)* **pumpkin ale** *or* **other beer**

1½ cups *or* **1** *(15-ounce)* **can canned pure pumpkin,** *NOT pumpkin pie filling*

2 tablespoons tomato paste

2 tablespoons Dijon mustard

2 tablespoons whole grain mustard

2 tablespoons seasoned rice vinegar

2 tablespoons dark molasses

3 cups chopped curly kale

Combine the flour, sage, salt, and pepper in a shallow dish or tin. Coat the ribs on all sides with the seasoned flour. Shake off excess.

Heat a large Dutch oven over high heat for 3 minutes. Add the canola oil; wait a minute or two, until the pan is very hot and almost smoking. Place the short ribs into the pan; sear until they are nicely browned on all three meaty sides. You will have to sear the meat in batches. Do not crowd the pot. Be patient; allow 4-5 minutes per side. When the ribs are nicely browned, transfer them to a plate to rest.

Reduce heat to medium; add the onion. Stir with a wooden spoon, scraping up all the browned bits in the pan. Cook 3-4 minutes, until the onion just starts to soften. Add 12 ounces of beer. Stir. Add the pumpkin. Stir in the tomato paste, Dijon mustard, whole grain mustard, vinegar, and molasses. Mix well. Bring sauce to a boil.

Return ribs to the pot. Stand them up if needed to fit all. Add the remaining 12 ounces of beer to almost cover the ribs. Add as much of the chopped kale as fits. Cover the pot. Simmer on low for 3 hours.

Transfer the ribs to a large platter. Spoon lots of braising juices over the ribs.

BEEF *carbonnade*

Witte beer is a Belgian-style ale that's very pale and cloudy in appearance because it is unfiltered and contains a high level of wheat. It is always spiced, generally with coriander, orange peel, and other background flavors. This dish is delicious and hearty, perfect for a fall or winter meal.

 YIELDS **6-8 SERVINGS**

2 tablespoons canola oil

4 pounds large flanken strips

3 **onions,** *peeled, halved, thinly sliced*

⅓ cup tomato paste

4 **cloves fresh garlic,** *sliced*

3 dried bay leaves

3 tablespoons all-purpose flour

3½ cups *(750 ml)* **Witte beer** *or other* **Belgian lager**

2 tablespoons dark brown sugar

2 tablespoons apple cider vinegar

2 **carrots,** *peeled, cut into 1-inch chunks*

1 cup beef *or* **chicken stock**

egg noodles, *cooked*

fresh parsley leaves

Heat a large Dutch oven or heavy pot over medium-high heat for 3 minutes. Add the canola oil; wait a minute or two, until the pan is very hot and almost smoking. Place the flanken strips into the pan; sear until meat is nicely browned on all 4 sides. You will have to sear the meat in batches. Do not crowd the pot. Be thorough, allowing them time to really caramelize. When the strips are nicely browned, transfer them to a plate to rest.

Add the onions, stirring with a wooden spoon to scrape up the browned bits from the bottom of the pot. Cook for 5-6 minutes, until beginning to caramelize; if starting to burn, reduce heat. Add the tomato paste. Stir. Add the garlic slices and bay leaves. Sprinkle in the flour; stir to make a thick onion roux mixture.

Pour in the beer. Stir to combine. Simmer for 2 minutes.

In a small bowl, combine the brown sugar and apple cider vinegar. Add to the pot along with the carrots.

Nestle the flanken back into the onions in the pot, bone-side up. Pour in any liquid that may have drained from the ribs onto the plate while they were resting. Add the stock. Reduce heat to medium-low. Simmer for 2 hours, uncovered. Remove from heat. Allow to cool in the pot for at least an hour.

Serve over egg noodles with lots of sauce and fresh parsley.

LAMB cholent "cassoulet"

Some of the most fun I have had in this career was being invited to judge cholent cook-offs from New York to California. The craziest entry was at the Yeshiva University competition, where one group entered a "S'mores cholent," graham crackers and marshmallows included. No gold medal there. Most memorable was a Shabbos I spent with my husband in San Diego to judge their event. The warmth of the community was exquisite and the creativity of the cholents was off the charts. They spanned a Moroccan version to a French lamb dish. I came home inspired and developed this recipe, which is an upscale rendition of the traditional.

 YIELDS **8-10 SERVINGS**

1½ pounds lamb cubes *or* **4 lamb shanks**

fine sea salt

freshly ground black pepper

1 tablespoon all-purpose flour

1 tablespoon canola oil

½ turnip, *not peeled, cut into 1-inch chunks*

½ bulb fennel, *top stalks removed and discarded, cut into 1-inch chunks*

2 carrots, *peeled, cut into 1-inch chunks*

1 onion, *peeled, cut into 1-inch dice*

3 cloves fresh garlic, *roughly chopped*

1 cup dry Northern beans

1 cup red wine

1 teaspoon dried thyme

1 teaspoon dried oregano

1 teaspoon kosher salt

½ teaspoon freshly ground black pepper

1 cup chopped kale

1 *(28-ounce)* **can crushed tomatoes**

7 cups beef broth

Line the bowl of a large slow cooker with a plastic liner. Season the lamb with salt and pepper. Dust the lamb with flour. Heat the oil in a large skillet. Sear the lamb in a single layer; if using shanks, use tongs to rotate them so you can brown them on all sides.

Place the lamb into the slow cooker. Add turnip, fennel, carrots, onion, garlic, beans, wine, thyme, oregano, salt, pepper, and kale. Add the crushed tomatoes. Fill the empty tomato can with beef broth; swish it around to get the remaining tomato; add broth to the pot. Add remaining broth. Push the kale down into the sauce.

Cover the slow cooker. Cook on low heat, 8 hours or overnight.

korean SHORT RIBS

I have done numerous shows in the Los Angeles area; each time I work there I reserve some time to explore a favorite spot, The Grove and the Original Farmers Market attached to it, established in 1934. It's a really fun culinary experience. While I was chatting with a vendor there, he recommended that I check out LA's Koreatown, the largest in the country. Talk about a sensory adventure! Since nothing there was kosher, I could hardly wait to call my chef friends for advice on making ribs. These hit the spot. Mix, dump, and cook. A simple recipe for a simply divine Asian-inspired dish. Remember to grab some napkins!

 YIELDS **8-10 SERVINGS**

5 pounds *(5 strips)* **breast flanken,** *not trimmed, cut into 2-3 bone sections*

3 tablespoons dark brown sugar

2 tablespoons red chili garlic sauce *or* **sambal oelek;** *I like Hung Foy brand*

¾ cup soy sauce

¼ cup water

10 very thin slices ginger, *not peeled, chopped, to make 2 tablespoons*

2 teaspoons garlic powder

1 tablespoon sesame oil

¼ cup ketchup

fresh scallion, *chopped, for garnish*

Place the ribs into a large (2-gallon) heavy-duty zip-lock bag. Sprinkle with brown sugar. In a medium bowl, stir together chili garlic sauce, soy sauce, water, ginger, garlic powder, and sesame oil. Pour into the bag. Rub it into all surfaces of the ribs. Marinate ribs in the refrigerator for 2 hours or overnight, the longer the better.

Preheat the oven to 350°F.

Place the ribs, meat-side down, in a casserole dish that fits them snugly in a single layer. Pour the marinade over the ribs. Cover with foil; bake 2½ hours.

Uncover the ribs. Carefully pour off 1½ cups of the pan juices; mix with the ketchup. Turn the ribs meat-side up. Pour and brush the mixture over the ribs. Transfer to serving platter; garnish with scallions.

spicy *kim chee* HANGAR STEAKS

True kim chee, a delicious Korean side dish, takes months to ferment properly. This quick kim chee gets better as it sits, so make a double batch. It is great on a burger or chicken breast.

 YIELDS **6-8 SERVINGS**

1 head Napa cabbage

1 teaspoon fine sea salt

1 teaspoon sugar

1 **carrot,** *peeled, minced into tiny ⅛-inch dice*

2 **scallions,** *root end trimmed, finely chopped*

1 **tablespoon fresh ginger,** *peeled, finely chopped*

½ teaspoon garlic powder

1 tablespoon sriracha

¼ cup mayonnaise

¼ **cup pickle juice,** *from any pickle that is not sweet*

3 **pounds** *(about 2)* **hangar steaks;** *have the butcher trim and remove the membrane; you should have 4 pieces*

1 tablespoon canola oil

Cut the head of cabbage into quarters lengthwise; chop into ¼-inch pieces. Place into a large bowl. Knead the salt and sugar into the cabbage to break it down. Add the carrot, scallions, ginger, garlic powder, and sriracha. Mix well; set aside.

In a small bowl, combine the mayonnaise and pickle juice. Brush on both sides of each steak.

Heat the oil in a grill pan until very hot but not smoking. Sear the steaks, 4-5 minutes per side for medium-rare. Allow the steaks to rest on a cutting board for 10 minutes. Slice steak; serve over the kim chee.

sloppy joe **PULLED BEEF** tacos

Pulled barbecue beef is all the rage right now in America. When the Wandering Que set up a pop-up shop in my neighborhood, the lines were two hours long and people were thrilled to wait on them, me included. Smoking meat is a process too arduous for a home-cook's easy dinner repertoire. I wrote this recipe to stand in for a simple Sloppy Joe saucy version of the pulled-beef sandwich. I love to wrap the leftovers in a flour tortilla with shredded lettuce, rice, and beans and eat them at room-temperature for lunch the next day.

 YIELDS **6-8 SERVINGS**

2-3 pounds second-cut brisket, *cut into 3 chunks*

½ teaspoon fine sea salt

½ teaspoon freshly ground black pepper

1 carrot, *peeled, cut into ¼-inch dice*

½ medium onion, *peeled, cut into ¼-inch dice*

1 *(28-ounce)* **can diced tomatoes,** *with their liquid*

1 teaspoon cumin

1 teaspoon dried oregano

1 teaspoon garlic powder

2 tablespoons dark brown sugar

3 tablespoons ketchup

2 tablespoons yellow mustard

8 taco shells

canned Sloppy Joe sauce, *warmed; I like Manwich*

Preheat the oven to 350°F.

Season the chunks of brisket on both sides with salt and pepper. Place into a 9 x 13-inch oven-to-table casserole dish that the meat fits into snugly. Sprinkle the carrot and onion over the top. Spread an even layer of the tomatoes with their liquid over the top.

In a small bowl, combine the cumin, oregano, and garlic powder. Stir in the brown sugar, ketchup, and mustard. Spoon over the top to distribute evenly.

Cover the dish; bake for 3 hours.

Transfer the meat to a cutting board, reserving pan juices. Using two forks, shred the beef. Return the meat to the dish, using pan juices to keep the meat moist. Fill the taco shells with the beef; drizzle with warm Sloppy Joe sauce.

TUSCAN square roast

In the weeks before teaching in Tuscany for the first time, I dreamed about the food, the ingredients, and the flavors that I would encounter. I surrounded myself with all things Italian. I wandered the streets of Arthur Avenue in the Bronx, the aisles of Eataly in New York, the shelves of travel books in Barnes and Noble. Then Shabbos came and I needed to cook a roast. Inspired by Italian fare, I developed this recipe, which has become a family favorite. The lightness of the ingredients allows the meat to shine without being masked by heavy wine flavors that sometimes dominate roasts.

 YIELDS **6-8 SERVINGS**

2 tablespoons extra-virgin olive oil

3 pounds **square roast** *or* **California roast**

1 *(12-ounce)* **jar marinated artichoke hearts,** *rinsed well and drained*

1 *(16-ounce)* **jar sweet red pepper slices,** *rinsed well and drained*

24 **fresh basil leaves**

8 **fresh garlic cloves,** *roughly chopped*

1 **medium onion,** *peeled, roughly chopped*

10 ounces *(about 30-35)* **cherry tomatoes,** *stems discarded*

1 teaspoon **dried basil**

1 teaspoon **dried oregano**

½ teaspoon **freshly ground black pepper**

¼ cup **tomato paste**

½ cup **white wine,** *such as Sauvignon Blanc or Pinot Grigio*

Heat the oil in a large pot over medium heat. Add the meat; sear for 4-6 minutes per side, until nicely browned. Using tongs, remove the meat to a plate or cutting board.

To the pot, add drained artichokes, red peppers, fresh basil, garlic, onion, tomatoes, dried basil, oregano, and pepper. Sauté for 5 minutes; stirring occasionally, until fragrant, scraping up the browned bits from the bottom of the pot. Return the meat to the pot. Add water to come halfway up on the roast.

In a small bowl, stir together tomato paste and wine. Pour over the meat. Cover the pot. Turn the heat to low; simmer, covered, for 3 hours.

Allow meat to cool. Transfer to a cutting board; slice against the grain, using a serrated knife. Using a slotted spoon, transfer the vegetables to a platter. Arrange the meat in the center. Return the heat to high; reduce the juices for 5-6 minutes to concentrate the flavor. Drizzle the roast with pan juices.

LASAGNA *bolognaise*

The Italian chefs that I worked with on all of my Italy trips needed to take a crash course on kosher. The goal of the Naomi Boutique travel program that I work for is to allow their guests to see, eat, and experience beautiful places around the world without compromise. To achieve that goal, they hire local chefs who, under the careful eye of a mashgiach, recreate local recipes using kosher ingredients. Within a day or two they are really in the swing of things and then Shabbos comes … with all of its rules that are very hard to explain to someone who has no idea and must be a quick study. In all parts of Italy, the chefs had chosen to include lasagna on the Shabbat day menus, which I found fascinating. Lasagna was never something I thought of as a Shabbos dish, but it really worked well and is now a dish that I have included in my own menu planning — to the delight of my guests.

 YIELDS **6 SERVINGS**

MEAT SAUCE

2 tablespoons extra-virgin olive oil

1 pound ground beef

4 cloves fresh garlic, *minced*

1 tablespoons dried oregano

¼ teaspoon red pepper flakes

1 teaspoon fine sea salt

½ teaspoon freshly ground black pepper

1 *(28-ounce)* can crushed tomatoes

1 cup red wine, *such as Cabernet Sauvignon or Chianti*

2 tablespoons tomato paste

BECHAMEL SAUCE

2 tablespoons unsalted margarine, *trans-fat-free if possible*

¼ cup all-purpose flour

2 cups plain, unsweetened soymilk or cashew milk, *not vanilla flavored*

12 lasagna noodles, *uncooked*

Preheat the oven to 425°F.

Prepare the meat sauce: Heat the oil in a large skillet over medium-high heat. Add the ground beef; cook for 5-6 minutes, until no longer pink, using a wooden spoon to break up the chunks. Add the garlic, oregano, red pepper flakes, salt, pepper, and crushed tomatoes. Pour the wine into the empty tomato can and swirl it around to pick up the remaining tomato on the sides of the can. Add to the pan. Add the tomato paste. Stir well; simmer for 10 minutes. Remove from heat.

Meanwhile, prepare the béchamel sauce: In a medium pot, melt margarine over low heat, allowing it to bubble. Add the flour and cook, raising the heat to medium, whisking the whole time until completely combined, about 1½ minutes. Do not allow it to brown. Gradually whisk in the soymilk, bring to a full boil, whisking constantly. Reduce heat to medium; simmer for 5 minutes, using a silicone spatula to scrape the bottom and sides of the pot. Remove from heat.

Place the lasagna noodles into a 9 x 13-inch oven-to-table casserole dish. Cover with very hot tap water. Soak for 5 minutes, agitating the noodles a few times to prevent sticking. Remove noodles to a clean kitchen towel; discard the water. Wipe out the pan, dry it, and coat with nonstick cooking spray.

In a small bowl, combine ¼ cup of the béchamel with ¼ cup of the meat sauce. Spread into the pan. Cover with 3 lasagna noodles, arranging them close but not overlapping. Spread with one-quarter of the meat sauce and then a thin layer of the béchamel sauce. Smooth with the back of a spoon. Cover with 3 more noodles. Repeat 2 more times, for a total of 4 layers of noodles and ending with the meat and béchamel sauces. Pour ¼ cup water into the meat skillet. Swirl to dredge up any remaining meat sauce. Pour into the pan, around the lasagna. Cover; bake for 30 minutes. Cool for 10 minutes; cut into pieces and serve.

Basher Fromagerie
Machane Yehuda Market, Jerusalem, Israel

Strawberries
Carpantras, France

Olive harvest, Sorrento, Italy

Parmigiano Reggiano cheese
Parma, Italy

Pasta making, Tuscany, Italy

Kal and Eric, Tuscany hilltops, Italy

Dairy / Fish

beresheet spa KANAFE

In 2014, when my Israel Foodie group was leaving the Beresheet Spa, after enjoying what might be the best breakfast buffet in Israel, I told Chef Boris Paukman that if he didn't share his Kanafe recipe, I would not be allowed back on the bus. He was lovely and accommodating. He made his in a 12-inch aluminum pan that looked like a pizza pan but he said it can be baked in a Pyrex pan or in a tart pan with removable bottom. It does not even have to be round, just shallow. Apollo, Athens, and Filo Factory package their kadaif, a shredded fillo dough that looks like thin noodles, in 1-pound boxes; use half the box.

 YIELDS **10 SERVINGS**

SIMPLE SYRUP

⅓ cup sugar

⅓ cup water

½ lemon

cinnamon stick

½ teaspoon rosewater

KANAFE

½ pound kadaif; *see note*

8 tablespoons unsalted butter, *melted, divided*

1 *(8-ounce)* block cream cheese

1 cup full-fat ricotta cheese

½ cup Tnuva brand Israeli Quark 91% fat free, *or* ½ cup full-fat sour cream

¾ cup sugar

chopped pistachios, *for garnish*

Prepare the simple syrup in advance: Place the sugar, water, lemon half, and cinnamon stick into a medium saucepan. Bring to a bubbling simmer; cook, uncovered, until it has reduced slightly and become thicker, 8-10 minutes. Remove from heat. Discard lemon and cinnamon stick. Stir in rosewater. Set aside to cool. Can be made ahead and stored in the fridge.

Preheat the oven to 350°F.

Place the kadaif into a bowl. Separate the strands. Add 5 tablespoons of the melted butter, reserving some for brushing the pan. Using your hands, toss strands to separate and coat with the melted butter.

Brush a 12-inch round aluminum pizza pan, tart pan, or 11-inch Pyrex pie plate with 1 tablespoon melted butter. Press in half the kadaif in an even layer, using your palms to spread it, covering the pan sides slightly.

In a stand mixer, combine the cream cheese, ricotta, Quark cheese, and sugar; don't make it too smooth, leave some lumps. Spread cheese mixture over the kadaif. Top with remaining kadaif. Brush with remaining melted butter, tucking kadaif edges into the pan.

Bake for 25 minutes. Broil for 2 minutes until it becomes a deep golden brown.

Drizzle the cold simple syrup onto the hot kanafe. Garnish with chopped pistachios.

KHACHAPURI *shakshuka*

Khachapuri is Georgian comfort food at its best. This boat-shaped delicacy is traditionally filled with a combination of tangy and gooey cheeses. Just before the bread hits your plate, an egg is added, which you stir into the cheese and devour before it has a chance to fully set. The ultimate place to sample this delicacy is a block off Machane Yehuda at Khachapuri Restaurant, which I do every time I visit Israel. Inspired, I came home to try to recreate the dish and swapped out the heavy cheese for the lighter and healthier shakshuka filling. Although not authentic, it brings me right back to a happy place with a calorie count that I can live with and the ability to prep in advance. In fact, I make a double batch of the shakshuka and freeze it, so all I have to do is pick up a ball of fresh pizza dough from my local pizza store or supermarket, and brunch or lunch is ready in a snap.

 OR **YIELDS 5 SERVINGS**

1 **onion,** *peeled*

1 **jalapeño pepper**

½ **green pepper**

6 **cloves fresh garlic,** *minced*

¼ **cup olive oil**

1 *(28-ounce)* **can crushed tomatoes**

¾ **cup water,** *plus more for thinning sauce*

¼ **cup tomato paste**

2 **teaspoons sweet** *or* **hot paprika**

½ **teaspoon fine sea salt**

¼ **teaspoon freshly ground black pepper**

1 **ball** *(1½ pounds)* **prepared pizza dough** *(enough to make a standard pie)*

½ **cup crumbled feta cheese,** *optional, for dairy meals*

5 **eggs**

chopped parsley, *for garnish*

Prepare the shakshuka: In the bowl of a food processor fitted with the metal "S" blade, chop the onion, jalapeño, green pepper, and garlic. Heat the oil in a large pot over medium heat. Add the vegetables; sauté until shiny and translucent, 8-10 minutes, or until fragrant.

Add the crushed tomatoes, ¾ cup water, tomato paste, paprika, salt, and pepper. Bring to a boil. Turn down heat; simmer for 15 minutes, adding water a tablespoon at a time if the sauce is too thick, stirring occasionally.

Preheat the oven to 450°F. Cover 1-2 cookie sheets with parchment paper. Set aside.

Cut the dough into 5 equal parts. Roll each into a rectangle or oval, ⅓-inch thick. Lay the dough on prepared cookie sheets. Roll each long side over itself and pinch each end to make a canoe shape. Use your fingers to spread the edges and stretch dough to make a space in the center for the shakshuka. Ladle some shakshuka into the center of each boat (you will have extra).

Bake for 10 minutes. Remove from the oven. Sprinkle with feta, if using for dairy meal. Crack 1 egg into the center of each boat. Return to oven until egg white is slightly set, 3-4 minutes. Garnish with chopped parsley.

fried **PIZZA** napolitana

Giuseppe Aversa, aka Chef Pepe, owns the glorious Il Buco restaurant in Sorrento, Italy. He is part artist, part chef, all around mensch. I was among the lucky ones in the summer of 2013 to work with him in Naomi Catering's kosher kitchen in the Hotel Grand Vesuvio on the Amalfi Coast. The chef came to one of my cooking shows to teach this pizza, a specialty of Naples. In his adorable broken English he taught us that Antico Molino Caputo "00" flour is the best for pizza and pasta. Indeed, it is the godfather of flours, with its finely ground powdery texture and low gluten for perfect crusts. Luckily, we can get it in the States. After schlepping bags of flour home in my luggage (my husband is an angel), I now buy mine at Fairway or online. Make sure to have extra for dusting your work surface.

 YIELDS **5 PIZZAS**

½ teaspoon instant *or* **rapid rise yeast**

2 teaspoons sugar

1⅓ cups warm *(not hot)* **water**

1 teaspoon salt

about 3 cups "00" flour; *see note*

1 tablespoon olive oil

canola oil

warm jarred marinara sauce

shredded mozzarella cheese

grated Parmesan cheese

fresh basil leaves, *for garnish*

In the bowl of stand mixer fitted with the dough hook, mix the yeast, sugar, and water. Add the salt. Slowly add the flour; mix for 2 minutes. With the machine running, drizzle in the oil. Knead for 7-8 minutes until a satiny dough forms, scraping down the sides as needed. Sometimes the last minute or two of kneading must be done by hand on your work surface to get the dough satiny. Alternatively, spread the flour into a circle, leaving the center open to make a well. Pour the water into the well; add the sugar and yeast. Gradually add in the flour by running your hand around the perimeter of the well, then slowly work the dough as to not heat and kill the yeast. Drizzle in drops of the oil and salt, kneading and adding flour as you continue the circular movements until a soft, satiny dough forms. Dust with more flour if needed, but do not use too much or the dough will be tough. Keep folding and kneading.

Form dough into a tight ball. Cover with a damp towel; allow the dough to rise at room temperature for 2-3 hours.

Preheat a pot or deep-fryer filled halfway with oil to 355-375°F. Preheat the oven to 500°F.

Divide the dough into 5 equal pieces; form each into a ball. Working with one piece at a time, slap the dough ball between your palms to start to work it. Place it on your floured work surface. Using your fingertips, knead, pat, and spread the dough into a flat round, about ¼-inch thick.

Fry the dough rounds, 1-2 minutes per side, turning with tongs. Remove when they are puffed and slightly golden. Place onto a cookie sheet. Return the oil to 355-375°F between rounds. Top the dough with warm marinara sauce, shredded mozzarella (not too much or crust will get soggy), and Parmesan. Bake until cheese is melted, 3-4 minutes. Garnish with fresh basil leaves.

meir adoni's
spinach ricotta **RAVIOLI**

The filling for this ravioli is delicious. If you are not going to make your own pasta dough, you can still make the filling and put it into a pastry or ziplock bag. Squeeze it into pasta shells or manicotti tubes that have been cooked al dente. Place on a shallow bed of marinara sauce, top with shaved Parmesan, and bake, covered, at 350°F for 10 minutes to heat through.

 YIELDS **20 RAVIOLI**

DOUGH

1¼ cups "00" flour *or* all-purpose flour

7 egg yolks from large eggs

1½ teaspoons extra-virgin olive oil

FILLING

9 ounces fresh baby spinach leaves, *washed well, but not dried*

15 ounces *(1½ cups)* ricotta cheese

1 tablespoon pine nuts, *plus additional for garnish, optional*

pinch ground nutmeg

1 teaspoon fresh lemon zest

¾ teaspoon salt

¼ teaspoon ground black pepper

olive oil

1 egg *and* 1 tablespoon water, *beaten together, for egg wash*

fine cornmeal *or* flour

Prepare the pasta dough: On a large clean work surface, pour the flour into a mound. Make a well in the center of the flour pile, forming walls around the well; make sure there is flour on the bottom so the egg yolks don't stick to the work area. Place the egg yolks and oil into the well. Using a fork, in a circular motion, stir wet ingredients just around rim of dry ingredients, bringing a bit of flour from the wall into the wet mixture a little at a time, until all are mixed together. Knead and fold the dough until it is elastic, soft, and smooth; this should take a full 10 minutes; if the dough is still very crumbly at the 5-minute mark, wet your hands with warm water. You may need to knead for a minute, wet your hands again, and continue kneading. If it is too wet, knead in a little more flour at a time until smooth and satiny. I find that a bench scraper is useful in helping to pick up and rotate the dough as I knead. Brush the surface with a little olive oil. Wrap the dough in plastic wrap; let it rest for 30 minutes at room temperature to relax the gluten.

Prepare the filling: Place the spinach into a heavy, high-sided pan. Cover; cook over medium heat for 5-6 minutes, shaking occasionally, until wilted. Drain, place into a kitchen towel or stack of paper towels, and squeeze out as much water as possible; then chop finely and transfer to a bowl. Add the ricotta, pine nuts, nutmeg, and lemon zest. Mix, seasoning with salt and pepper. Put into a pastry bag or ziplock bag with the end snipped. Set aside.

Cut the ball of dough into quarters. To keep them from drying out, cover and reserve the pieces you are not using. Dust the counter with flour. Leave yourself plenty of room. Press the dough into a flat rectangle and roll it through a pasta machine, 2-3 times, at widest setting. Pull and stretch the sheet of dough as it emerges from the rollers. Reduce the setting and crank the dough through again, 2-3 times, until the dough is very thin. If you don't have a pasta machine, you can do this with a rolling pin but it will be more difficult and take much longer. The dough should be thin enough so that you can almost see your countertop though it.

With a 3¼-inch round biscuit cutter or cookie cutter, cut out circles of dough. Pipe filling onto the center of one round, leaving a border of dough so filling won't ooze out while cooking. Brush egg wash around the edge of the filling. Carefully lay a second pasta round on top. Press down around the edges to seal the pasta and gently press out air pockets around the filling. Repeat this process with remaining dough. Dust the ravioli and cookie sheet with flour or cornmeal to prevent pasta from sticking; allow them to dry slightly while assembling the rest.

Cook the ravioli in boiling salted water for 4 minutes. Cook in batches; do not overcrowd the pot. They will float to the top when ready. Lift them out with a spider or slotted spoon. Serve plain or over warm marinara. Garnish with additional pine nuts.

BUTTERNUT SQUASH *farroto*

All the deliciousness of risotto but none of the work! Farro is a chewy, earthy whole-grain that is grown in Tuscany. When stirred like risotto, it releases its starch to obtain a creamy result. My family likened this dish to a grown-up Mac 'n Cheese.

 YIELDS **6-8 SERVINGS**

1 pound butternut squash, *peeled, cut into chunks*

olive oil

fine sea salt

freshly ground black pepper

1 pound semi-pearled farro

vegetable stock *(for homemade, see below)*

6 ounces Grana Padano or **Parmigiano Reggiano,** *grated*

4 tablespoons unsalted butter, *cut into chunks*

8-10 fresh sage leaves, *chopped*

Preheat the oven to 350°F. Line a cookie sheet with parchment paper. Season the squash with olive oil, salt, and pepper. Roast the squash until soft and you are able to pierce it with a fork, about 40 minutes. Transfer roasted squash to a food processor fitted with the metal "S" blade. Purée the squash.

Meanwhile, place the farro into an 8-quart pot. Cover with vegetable stock by an inch or two. Bring to a boil over high heat; reduce heat, cover, and simmer until al dente, about 18 minutes.

Add puréed squash, stirring it to achieve a risotto consistency. Add more stock as needed. Finish by stirring in the grated cheese and butter. Stir in the chopped sage. Serve immediately

VEGETABLE *stock*

10 cups water	**large handful parsley stems**	**1 dried bay leaf**
2 carrots, *peeled*	**large handful dill stems**	**large pinch kosher salt**
2 ribs celery	**handful basil stems**	**3 whole black peppercorns**
1 large white onion, *peeled, halved*	**woody stems from one bunch asparagus**	**½ small red chili,** *optional*

Place the water, carrots, celery, onion, parsley, dill, basil, asparagus stems, bay leaf, salt, peppercorns, and chili, if using, into a large pot. Bring to a boil; allow to simmer until reduced by half. This will take about a half-hour. Strain stock; discard the vegetables. You will have more than enough for this recipe. Make a double batch and keep some on hand in your fridge or freezer for future use.

strawberry *mascarpone*
BREAD PUDDING

When working in Provence, France, my favorite days were market days. Rows and rows of vendors fill the streets with their wares. It is a bombardment of the senses. Heady fragrance of herbs, soaps, lavender, honey, olives, and so much more fill the air. Local bands play their tunes. Linens, table-cloths, knives, candles, bowls — all on display. One favorite market town was Carpentras, home to a gorgeous 14th-century synagogue and the world's most famous strawberries. This recipe is an ode to those red jewels whose taste stays in my memory banks. This dish is where dairy kugel meets challah soufflé meets bread pudding meets heaven.

If you only have a 9 x 13-inch pan, you may need to use the additional ½ challah.

 YIELDS **10-12 SERVINGS**

12 ounces mascarpone cheese

¾ cup strawberry jam

1-1½ *(15-18 ounce)* **store-bought egg challahs,** *crusts trimmed as best you can*

6 large eggs

¾ cup half & half

¼ teaspoon freshly ground black pepper

1 cup whole cornflake cereal

4 tablespoons unsalted butter

¼ cup dark brown sugar

3-4 fresh strawberries, *chopped*

Preheat the oven to 350°F. Spray an 8 x 11-inch oval oven-to-table pan with nonstick cooking spray. Set aside.

In a medium bowl, stir the mascarpone with the jam until just blended.

Cut the trimmed challah in half lengthwise. Cut a pocket the entire length of the challah half, making sure not to cut all the way through. Fill each half with half of the strawberry mascarpone. Cut each half into large cubes or chunks. Place into the prepared pan, making 2 layers, stuffing in chunks to fill any gaps.

In a medium bowl, whisk the eggs, half & half, and pepper. Slowly drizzle over the challah in the pan, allowing egg mixture to soak into the bread, stopping every few seconds to compact the bread with your palms and help it absorb the egg.

Place the cornflakes into a small bowl. In a small skillet, melt the butter and brown sugar, stirring frequently. When mixture is smooth, pour it over the cornflakes. Use a wooden spoon to toss together; be careful, it will be hot. Sprinkle over the top of the soufflé. Toss the chopped strawberries on top. Cover with foil. Bake, covered, for 30 minutes. Uncover and bake 20 minutes.

spinach artichoke **PASTA** *fritatta*

This is the Italian way to use up last night's pasta. I use spaghetti but you can use any shape pasta. You can even use pasta if it was sauced, as long as you don't include too much of the sauce so the frittata will hold together.

On our day trips in Italy, we always packed a picnic lunch. Frittatas, quiches, and grain salads were the perfect components, since they are all great at room temperature and easy to tote around.

You can add anything to a frittata: fresh herbs, salmon, tuna, or any cooked vegetables that you have on hand.

D   YIELDS **4-6 SERVINGS**

4 ounces spaghetti *or* ½ pound cooked leftover spaghetti

2 tablespoons unsalted butter

2 tablespoons extra-virgin olive oil

6 cloves fresh garlic, *minced*

6 ounces baby spinach

3-4 frozen artichoke bottoms, *defrosted, cut into ½-inch dice*

1 cup grated Parmesan cheese

½ cup heavy cream

2 ounces block cream cheese

5 large eggs

¼ teaspoon fine sea salt

¼ teaspoon freshly ground black pepper

Preheat the oven to 400°F.

If you are preparing the pasta fresh for this dish, cook it in salted water according to package directions until al dente. Drain. Set aside.

In a heavy, nonstick, 12-inch ovenproof skillet, over medium heat, melt the butter with the olive oil. Swirl to distribute it around the whole bottom of the pan. Add the garlic, spinach, and artichokes. Sauté for 4-5 minutes, making sure the garlic doesn't brown; if it starts to brown, lower the heat. Cook until the spinach is cooked down. Add in the Parmesan, heavy cream, and cream cheese; cook for additional 2 minutes.

Meanwhile, in a medium bowl, whisk the eggs with the salt and pepper. Turn the heat to medium-low. Add the cooked pasta and the eggs to the pan, spreading the eggs so they are evenly distributed. Cook for 10 minutes over medium-low until the mixture is firm on the bottom. Shake the pan to make sure the frittata is not sticking. Transfer the skillet to the oven; bake for 10 minutes. Transfer to a plate, cut into wedges, and serve warm or at room temperature.

cheesy GRITS casserole

Having a daughter study at Emory University in Atlanta, Georgia meant heading down south on multiple occasions. Grits are a Southern culinary tradition. They are small broken grains of corn that are cooked into a luscious breakfast delicacy or dinner side dish. Hot cereal was always a big hit when my kids were young, so I knew they would love this creamy rendition; the rich addition of egg just puts it over the top.

 YIELDS **6 SERVINGS**

2 cups heavy cream

6 cups water

1½ teaspoons fine sea salt, *divided*

2 cups corn grits *or* **stone-ground polenta**

1 cup shredded mozzarella cheese

1 cup ricotta cheese

6 large eggs

½ cup shredded cheddar cheese

3 tablespoons grated Parmesan cheese

Preheat the oven to 350°F. Spray a 9 x 13-inch casserole dish with nonstick cooking spray. Set aside.

Select a large, deep pot to allow the grits to bubble without splattering while they cook. Place the pot over medium-low heat; mix in the cream, water, and 1 teaspoon salt. Heat the liquid to warm, but not boiling. Stirring the whole time to prevent lumps, add the grits.

Cook 8-10 minutes, stirring occasionally, until creamy and bubbles make small volcanoes in the grits. Turn off the heat.

Quickly stir in the mozzarella, ricotta, and ½ teaspoon salt. Transfer to prepared casserole dish. Smooth the top. Wait 5 minutes for the grits to set. Using the back of a spoon, make 6 indentations at even intervals. Crack an egg into each indentation. Sprinkle with cheddar and Parmesan. Bake, uncovered, for 10 minutes for soft-set eggs. Serve immediately.

trio of ROSÉ PASTA

There is nothing more indulgent than a big bowl of pasta in a creamy tomato sauce. Cut down your guilty conscience and your waistline by making this dish as a trio of pasta, zucchini noodles, and spaghetti squash that looks like noodles! Fun and delicious for the whole family.

 YIELDS **8-10 SERVINGS**

1 **medium spaghetti squash**

2 **zucchini,** *not peeled*

1 **tablespoon water**

1 **pound penne pasta,** *cooked according to package directions until al dente, drained*

3 **tablespoons unsalted butter**

2 **tablespoons extra-virgin olive oil**

1 **small onion,** *minced*

4 **large cloves garlic,** *each cut in half*

¼ **teaspoon dried oregano**

¼ **teaspoon dried basil**

¼ **teaspoon crushed red pepper flakes**

½ **cup rosé** *or* **white wine**

1 *(28-ounce)* **can whole plum tomatoes,** *with their liquid*

1 **cup heavy whipping cream**

½ **teaspoon salt**

1 **cup grated Parmesan cheese**

black pepper

Place a rack in the center of the oven; preheat to 350°F.

Place the spaghetti squash directly on the oven rack; bake for 45-60 minutes. Check for doneness after 45 minutes by depressing the sides; they should yield slightly. Cook up to 1 hour as needed. Set aside.

Using a spiral slicer (Spiralizer), cut the zucchini into spaghetti-like noodles. Cut spirals into about 3-inch pieces. Place into microwave-safe bowl with water. Cover with plastic wrap; microwave for 3 minutes. Place into a large serving bowl. Set aside.

Place cooked pasta into a second large serving bowl.

Meanwhile, heat the butter and oil in a large pot over medium heat. Add the onion, garlic, oregano, basil, and crushed red pepper flakes; sauté 3 minutes. Add the wine. Add tomatoes and their liquid; with a gloved hand, squeeze the tomatoes in the pot to break them open. Simmer for 15 minutes, stirring occasionally, or until liquid evaporates. Using an immersion blender, process until sauce reaches desired consistency.

Stir in cream and salt. Simmer for 10 minutes, stirring frequently. Add Parmesan cheese, mixing well. Season with pepper to taste.

Cut the spaghetti squash in half. Scoop out and discard the seeds. Using a fork, pull apart spaghetti-like strands of squash; place them into third serving bowl.

Divide sauce among the bowls of penne, squash, and zucchini, tossing to coat. Serve immediately.

RISOTTO *alla milanese*

Risotto was a gift from the Jews to Italy. During the Middle Ages, the Arabs introduced rice to Italy through Sicily, where many Jews lived. When the Spanish edict of expulsion came in 1492, Naples, Sicily — all of south Italy — were under Spanish control. The Sephardic Sicilian exiles fled north and took risotto with them. Later, rice cultivation moved to the rich soil of the Po Valley in northern Italy, and rice became the preferred staple —even more than pasta. Italian Jews prepared risottos loaded with every kind of vegetable, meat, and giblet since they could not afford to waste any part of the chicken, and it is still prepared on Fridays for Shabbat dinner in a dish called "Riso Sabbath col zafran" — "Sabbath rice with saffron."

Saffron is one of the most precious spices in the world, retailing for more than $500 an ounce. It consists of the dried stigmas of the purple crocus. The expense comes from the extraordinary labor involved in harvesting and preparing it for storage. There are only 3 stigmas or saffron threads per flower. Eighty thousand flowers are needed to obtain one pound of saffron.

Risotto alla Milanese is one of the most famous dishes in Lombardy's culinary tradition. Although it is traditionally made with saffron, Grana Padano cheese, and bone marrow, as kosher cooks, we leave out the marrow bone. To switch it up, you can omit the dairy and instead roast marrow bones to serve in the saffron-rich rice.

  YIELDS **6 SERVINGS**

2 **tablespoons canola oil,** *plus more for frying sage leaves*

1 **onion,** *peeled, diced into ¼-inch pieces*

1 **clove fresh garlic,** *minced*

2 **cups Arborio, Carnaroli,** *or* **Vialone Nano rice**

large pinch of saffron threads

½ **cup white wine**

4 **cups water** *or* **vegetable stock**

1 **tablespoon butter**

1 **cup grated Grana Padano** *or* **Parmesan cheese**

fine sea salt, *to taste*

sage leaves, *for garnish*

Heat the 2 tablespoons oil in an 8-quart pot. Add the onion; cook until translucent, but do not allow it to brown, 6-7 minutes. Add the garlic; cook for 1 minute.

Add the rice; toast it for 2 minutes. Stir in the saffron, toasting it for 2 minutes. Add the wine. Add the water or stock, 1 cup at a time, allowing it to absorb each time, slowly simmering and stirring the rice. You may need 1-2 additional cups of water depending on how dry the risotto becomes. Time will vary based on heat source, but rice should be cooked in 35-45 minutes.

Meanwhile, heat a bit of canola oil in a small pan. Drop in the sage leaves; when they stop snapping they are done, about 30 seconds. Remove from pan; set aside.

When the rice is creamy, add the butter, cheese, and salt to taste. Stir until velvety. Ladle into bowls. Garnish with fried sage leaves. Serve immediately.

silan glazed SALMON
with date *and chickpea salad*

We can never have enough salmon recipes, and with salmon's health benefits, that's a great thing. Here's a new one that is off the charts and a snap to prepare. The silan keeps the fish moist, flavorful, and luscious. The salad makes it exotic, fancy, and festive.

 YIELDS **6-8 SERVINGS**

6 *(6-8 ounce)* **salmon fillets**

silan *(date syrup)*

1 *(15-ounce)* **can chickpeas,** *rinsed and drained*

1 cup *(8-9)* **Medjool dates,** *pits removed and discarded*

1 stalk celery, *cut into ¼-inch dice*

3 red radishes, *cut into ¼-inch dice*

½ small red onion, *peeled, cut into very thin julienne slices*

6 mint leaves, *finely chopped*

¼ cup extra-virgin olive oil, *plus additional for plating*

¼ teaspoon fine sea salt

⅛ teaspoon freshly ground black pepper

zest and juice of ½ orange

⅓ cup fresh parsley leaves, *chopped*

Preheat the oven to 350°F.

Line a cookie sheet with parchment paper. Lay the salmon fillets on the parchment; do not allow them to touch. Brush each with a thin coat of silan on all sides. Bake, uncovered, for 12 minutes. Remove from oven and brush on a thicker coating of silan. Return salmon to the oven and bake for a final 5 minutes or until almost cooked in the center at the thickest part.

Meanwhile, place the chickpeas into a large bowl. Slice, then dice the dates; add them to the bowl. Add the celery, radishes, onion, and mint. Drizzle in the ¼ cup olive oil. Sprinkle in the salt, pepper, orange zest, juice, and parsley. Toss well to evenly dress and distribute the ingredients.

Scoop the date salad onto a serving platter or individual plates. Top with salmon. Drizzle a little olive oil and additional silan around the plate.

COD AL FORNO
with *roasted tomatoes*

This recipe is where my Italian food brain met my Israeli one. Al forno is Italian for "in the oven." The tomatoes and garlic are a great match for the clean flavor of the cod. The Israeli couscous creates a playful crust that allows me to use a quintessential Israeli product in a new way.

 YIELDS **4 SERVINGS**

2 *(2 pounds)* **large cod fillets, each cut in half**

4 **beefsteak tomatoes** *(plus one additional, if desired, for garnish)*

½ cup **extra-virgin olive oil,** *divided*

6-8 **cloves fresh garlic,** *each thinly sliced lengthwise*

1½ cups **water**

½ teaspoon **salt,** *plus more for seasoning the fish*

1 cup **Israeli** *(pearl)* **couscous**

½ teaspoon **dried parsley**

½ teaspoon **dried basil**

½ teaspoon **dried oregano**

freshly ground black pepper

Preheat oven to 300°F. Cover a large cookie sheet with parchment paper. Set aside.

Slice each tomato into ½-inch slices; cut out the core, if possible. Place onto prepared sheet. Drizzle with 3 tablespoons olive oil. Place one garlic slice into the center of each tomato slice. Scatter any remaining garlic over the tomatoes. Roast, uncovered, for 2 hours. Remove from oven; cool.

Raise oven temperature to 450°F.

Transfer the tomatoes to a cutting board. Using a sharp knife, chop them to make a chunky paste; discard any hard parts of the core. Reserve 4 slices, if desired, for garnish. Set aside.

Bring water with ½ teaspoon salt to a boil. Add the couscous. Cover, turn down the heat, and simmer for 8 minutes. Remove from heat. Stir in the remaining olive oil, parsley, basil, and oregano.

Line the cookie sheet with a fresh piece of parchment paper. Place the cod on the parchment. Season with salt and pepper. Top the cod with a thick coating of the roasted tomatoes. Top with the couscous. Cover loosely with foil. Roast, covered, for 8 minutes; remove foil and roast a final 4 minutes.

Allow the cod to rest. Transfer to individual plates or serving platter. Garnish some of the portions with a slice of roasted tomato and garlic, optional.

citrus *poached* SALMON

I treasure my poaching pan. My kind, generous, and thoughtful father-in-law bought me mine at Zabar's 20 years ago, after I mentioned that I wanted to learn how to poach fish. It is designed to immerse a long piece of fish in liquid. The handles make the delicate cooked fish easy to remove from the pan and a cinch to transfer to a platter in one piece after cooking. The elevated bottom keeps the fish from cooking too quickly against the direct heat of the pan. If you don't have a poaching pan, drape a large, double layer of cheesecloth in your roasting pan and place the fish in the center of it. Twist the ends to create makeshift handles that can be used to lift the fish out of the liquid when it's done cooking. Cover the pan tightly with foil.

 YIELDS **8-10 SERVINGS**

CITRUS MAYO

1 lime

1 navel orange

⅓ cup mayonnaise

1 lemon

1 teaspoon Dijon mustard

1 teaspoon honey

POACHED SALMON

½ **cup orange juice,** *not from concentrate*

½ **cup white wine,** *such as Sauvignon Blanc*

1 *(3-4 pound)* **side of salmon with skin,** *pin bones removed*

½ **teaspoon fine sea salt**

¼ **teaspoon freshly ground black pepper**

½ **bunch** *(6-8 stems)* **fresh dill,** *root ends trimmed, rinsed well*

½ **bunch** *(6-8 stems)* **fresh cilantro,** *root ends trimmed, rinsed well*

1 **English hothouse cucumber,** *not peeled*

Preheat the oven to 350°F.

Prepare the citrus mayo: Zest half the lime and half the orange. Thinly slice the partially zested fruits; set aside. Stir the lime zest and orange zest into the mayonnaise. Add 1 teaspoon juice from the lemon; slice the lemon. Set it aside with the other sliced citrus. Stir the mustard and honey into the mayonnaise. Store in refrigerator until ready to use.

Prepare the salmon: Pour the orange juice and wine into the poacher. Place the salmon into the poacher. Season with salt and pepper. Scatter the lime, orange, and lemon slices over the fish. Top with dill and cilantro. Cover the poacher; bake for 35 minutes or until just opaque in the center.

Cool for a few minutes. Discard all the citrus, dill, and cilantro. Carefully transfer the salmon to large platter; it is okay if the skin remains in the poacher. Refrigerate until cold, or up to a day ahead.

When ready to serve, using a handheld mandolin on the finest setting, shave paper-thin slices of cucumber.

Spread the citrus mayo in an even layer over the fish. Arrange the cucumber in overlapping columns on the mayo.

TILAPIA
with *browned butter caper sauce*

In Israel, St. Peter's fish is quite popular. Here in the United States, it is known as tilapia and is also a crowd-pleaser with its soft texture and non-fishy taste. In the recent past, tilapia farms had earned an unsavory reputation for bad environmental practices and other unhealthy actions that resulted in unhealthy fish. A growing number of tilapia farms are now receiving third-party certification from such organizations as the Global Aquaculture Alliance. Tilapia from America, Canada, and Ecuador are "best choices." Talk to your fishmonger to ensure you are getting healthy fish, raised in an environmentally sound way, and then ... fire up your frying pan, because this simple dish will knock your socks off.

 YIELDS **4 SERVINGS**

4 *(6-ounce)* **tilapia fillets**

4 **tablespoons butter,** *plus more for greasing pan*

¼ **cup white wine**

2 **tablespoons fresh lemon juice**

2 **cloves fresh garlic,** *minced*

2 **tablespoons capers,** *rinsed and drained*

½ **teaspoon dried oregano**

¼ **teaspoon fine sea salt**

fresh chopped parsley, *for garnish*

Preheat the oven to 425°F.

Lightly grease a baking dish with butter; be sure it is large enough to hold the fish in a single layer. Place the fish into the dish.

In a small pan, over low heat, melt 4 tablespoons butter until it turns foamy, is light brown in color, and has a nutty aroma, about 5 minutes. Remove from heat. Swirl in the wine, lemon juice, garlic, capers, oregano, and salt; pour over the fillets.

Bake, uncovered, for 10-15 minutes, or until fish flakes easily with a fork. Garnish with chopped parsley.

herbed HALIBUT and white beans

A trip to the farmers' market for fresh herbs, a stop at the fish store, a bottle of white wine, and a long summer evening dining out on your deck. That's what this dish conjures up for me — although I have been known to enjoy it all year long.

 YIELDS **4 SERVINGS**

3 fresh sage leaves

4 fresh basil leaves

¼ cup fresh parsley leaves

½ teaspoon dried rosemary

1 clove fresh garlic

fine sea salt

freshly ground black pepper

¼ cup extra-virgin olive oil, *plus additional for cooking and finishing*

1½ pounds *(1 large)* **halibut fillet,** *with skin*

4 tablespoons butter

1 *(15-ounce)* **can Great White Northern beans,** *rinsed and drained*

Place the sage, basil, parsley, rosemary, garlic, ¼ teaspoon salt, and ¼ teaspoon pepper into the bowl of a food processor fitted with the metal "S" blade. Pulse, scraping down the sides. With the machine running, slowly drizzle in the ¼ cup olive oil.

Season the fish with salt and pepper. In a large skillet (big enough to hold the fish and the beans), over medium heat, melt the butter and 2-3 tablespoons olive oil. Sear the fish, skin-side up, for 4 minutes. Using a fish turner, flip the fish. Add the beans to the pan. Stir the herbs into the beans; brush a little onto the top of the fish fillet. Cook until the fish is no longer opaque in the center, 3-4 minutes; do not overcook.

Spoon the beans onto a platter; top with the fish. Drizzle with olive oil.

chef michael katz's FISH KEBABS

One of the perks of leading a culinary tour to Israel is meeting many prominent chefs. One of my favorites, Chef Michael Katz, is so sweet, I can only describe him with the Yiddish word "aidle." He is executive chef of the Adom Group, among the best restaurants in Israel. Our stop was Trattoria Haba, outside the shuk. Michael treated us to a demo, including this dish, which we devoured. To listen to Michael is to learn through food about science, history, art, love, and life in Israel.

Michael used ras el hanut, a local spice blend made of approximately 15 spices. Pick up some next time you are in the shuk. I subbed in spices easier to find here in the States.

The main "secret" is to chop all the fish by hand and not with a meat grinder or a food processor. This keeps the proteins from becoming a sticky mass. I say, leave it to the professionals with the razor-sharp knives, and have the fishmonger chop it for you to make prep work a snap.

 D OR **P**   YIELDS **4 SERVINGS**

½ **pound tilapia fillet,** *cut into ½-inch dice*

½ **pound cod fillet,** *cut into ½-inch dice*

⅓ **cup unflavored breadcrumbs**

1 **tablespoon pine nuts**

¼ **teaspoon cumin**

¼ **teaspoon smoked paprika**

¼ **teaspoon chili pepper**

¼ **teaspoon schwarma spice** *or* **ras el hanut**

¼ **teaspoon baking soda**

¼ **teaspoon salt**

¼ **teaspoon freshly ground black pepper**

2 **fresh cloves garlic,** *minced*

1 **tablespoon chopped fresh curly parsley**

1 **tablespoon chopped fresh cilantro leaves**

1 **scallion,** *chopped, white and pale green parts only*

¼ **small white onion,** *peeled, finely chopped*

extra-virgin olive oil

techina, yogurt, *or* **tartar sauce,** *for serving*

Place the diced fish into a medium bowl. Add the breadcrumbs, pine nuts, cumin, smoked paprika, chili powder, schwarma spice, baking soda, salt, pepper, garlic, parsley, cilantro, scallion, and onion. Mix gently. Oil your hands with olive oil. Knead the mass until it combines and holds together, but don't over-knead or the fish will be chewy. If it won't hold together well, sprinkle in a little more breadcrumb.

Dampen your hands. Divide mixture into 8 portions; shape each into a kebab form, like a small egg. Heat a thin layer of olive oil in a medium skillet over medium heat. Cook the kebabs until golden on all sides, 4-6 minutes total, turning until colored on all sides and cooked through.

Serve 2 kebabs per plate with techina, yogurt, or tartar sauce.

porcini *crusted* SEA BASS

We saw farmers selling fresh porcini mushrooms on the side of the road in Italy. That doesn't happen very often here in Livingston, New Jersey, so my ode to the porcini comes by way of the dried form, pulverized to a powder. A coffee or spice grinder yields perfect powdery results. It makes an incredible crusting for fish for a complete dinner that is on the table in 10 minutes!

 YIELDS **4 SERVINGS**

1 ounce dried porcini mushrooms

¼ teaspoon fine sea salt

⅛ teaspoon freshly ground black pepper

4 *(6-8 ounce)* **thick portions Chilean sea bass, halibut** *or* **red snapper fillets**

½ cup extra-virgin olive oil

12 cloves fresh garlic, *minced*

12 ounces fresh baby spinach leaves

Place the dried mushrooms into a coffee or spice grinder. This can also be done in the bowl of a food processor fitted with the metal "S" blade or in a blender. Process until a powder forms. Remove to a shallow bowl; stir in the salt and pepper.

Press each fish fillet into the porcini mixture to coat and crust one side. Set aside.

Place the oil and garlic into a very large (14-inch) skillet; turn the heat to medium. Cook for 45-60 seconds, until the garlic is fragrant. Add the spinach, tossing with tongs, to sauté as it quickly cooks down, about 2 minutes. Remove to a bowl. Discard any liquid emitted by the spinach.

Add the fish to the skillet, crust-side down; sear for 3 minutes. Turn fish; cook for 3-4 minutes, depending on thickness, until the fish is cooked through. Use tongs to place spinach on a platter, leaving liquid in the bowl. Serve fish over the spinach.

Testing balsamic vinegar, Modena, Italy

Orange groves, Florida

Spice market, Mexico

Dried fruit at the Shuk, Jerusalem, Israel

Market day, Provence, France

Lavender fields near Gordes, France

Side Dishes

sweet and sour RATATOUILLE

Attending the bar mitzvah of the son of a lifelong best friend is an emotional moment. Celebrating with the parade of their relatives whom you have seen woven in and out of life over many years, the child's grandparents whom you knew yourself as a child, and of course seeing all that your friend has accomplished, are all reasons to be full of emotion and happiness. I enjoyed this experience at my friend Dr. Shari Mann's simchah. Between that, and this incredible ratatouille that Greenwald Caterers graciously shared with me, it was a perfect weekend.

 YIELDS **10 SERVINGS**

5 **yellow squash,** *not peeled, each cut in half lengthwise*

5 **zucchini,** *not peeled, each cut in half lengthwise*

2 **red bell peppers**

olive oil-flavored nonstick cooking spray

1 **tablespoon canola oil**

1 **large onion,** *peeled, cut into ½-inch dice*

1 *(12-ounce)* **can tomato paste**

½ **cup white vinegar**

5 **tablespoons dark brown sugar**

3 **tablespoons sugar**

1 **tablespoon lemon juice**

2 **tablespoons garlic powder**

1 **tablespoon onion powder**

1 **teaspoon salt**

1 **teaspoon turmeric**

½ **teaspoon black pepper**

Preheat the oven to 375°F. Line 2 jellyroll pans with parchment paper.

Using a melon baller or rounded teaspoon, scrape out the seeds of the squash, zucchini, and peppers. Cut veggies into bite-sized pieces. Place on prepared pans. Coat with cooking spray. Roast, uncovered, for 20 minutes.

Meanwhile, heat the oil in a large pot. Sauté onion over medium heat until fragrant and slightly golden, 5-6 minutes.

Add the tomato paste to the pot. Fill can with boiling water, stirring to pick up any remaining tomato, and add to the pot. Add 2 more cans of water. Add the vinegar, brown sugar, sugar, lemon juice, garlic powder, onion powder, salt, turmeric, and black pepper. Bring to a simmer.

Add the semi-roasted vegetables. Cover pot; cook on low for 45 minutes.

EGGPLANT *and* tomato tart

Each morning, when my tour group left to explore Provence, we left laden with goodies for a picnic lunch. The picnic always included salad, a fish dish, a grain, and a different version of Pissaliediere. Pissaliediere is the French flaky cousin to pizza, which is traditionally topped with olives and caramelized onions. I love this version with eggplant and olives, but feel free to change up the toppings. For a dairy meal, you could add some feta cheese to the olive mixture.

 YIELDS **9 SERVINGS**

1 small eggplant, *cut into paper-thin (¹⁄₁₆-inch) slices using a hand-held mandolin or very sharp knife*

extra-virgin olive oil

½ teaspoon fine sea salt

⅛ teaspoon freshly ground black pepper

1 teaspoon dried oregano

¾ cup *(about 12)* **thinly sliced grape tomatoes**

⅓ cup packed *(about 18)* **Kalamata olives,** *pitted, very finely chopped*

2 cloves fresh garlic, *minced*

1 sheet puff pastry, *at room temperature for 20 minutes*

1 teaspoon tomato paste

fresh basil leaves, *torn, for garnish*

Preheat the oven to 425°F. Line a baking sheet with parchment paper; coat with nonstick cooking spray.

Place the eggplant slices into a large bowl. Coat with ¼ cup olive oil. Sprinkle on salt, pepper, and oregano. Add the tomatoes. Use both hands to toss and coat the slices well. Set aside.

Place the olives, garlic, and 1 tablespoon olive oil into a small bowl. Mix well.

Place the sheet of puff pastry on the prepared baking sheet; open pastry sheet but don't roll it out. Spread an even layer of the olive mixture over the pastry, leaving just a small border on all sides. Cover the olive mixture with columns of overlapping slices of the eggplant. Scatter the tomatoes over the eggplant.

In a small bowl, combine tomato paste and 1 teaspoon olive oil. Using a pastry brush, gently dab this all over the tart and on the edges of the pastry. Cover the edges with strips of foil to prevent burning.

Bake, uncovered, for 20 minutes; don't open the oven door during baking.

Remove from oven. Toss some torn basil leaves over the top; drizzle with olive oil.

TERSHI *and* couscous

Chef Meir Adoni is the face of Israeli cuisine today. He taught me this dish, a pumpkin dip from the Libyan Jewish community — a dish he uses to impress his own mother-in-law. He always has a supply of preserved lemons on hand. I do not, so I take a seedless lemon, microwave it for 1½ minutes, cut it in half, and throw it into the food processor with ½ teaspoon kosher salt. I pulse it a few times before using and it adds a great bright acidic note. Preserved lemons can be purchased online.

 YIELDS **6-8 SERVINGS**

4 pounds pumpkin *or* **Kabocha squash,** *cut into large chunks, seeds removed*

olive oil

2 Italian eggplants

½ teaspoon smoked paprika

½ teaspoon sweet paprika

½ teaspoon fine sea salt

¼ teaspoon cumin

⅛ teaspoon cayenne pepper

¼ cup chopped preserved *or* **pickled lemon** *(see note above)*

½ jalapeño pepper

8 cloves fresh garlic

2 cups prepared couscous

Preheat the oven to 450°F. Line a baking sheet with parchment paper.

Place the pumpkin, skin-side down, on prepared pan. Drizzle with olive oil; then rub to coat each chunk. Roast until soft; time will differ based on size of chunks, but the range is 25-40 minutes. Allow to cool.

To minimize mess, lift your stove grates and cover the stove with foil. Replace the grates. Place the eggplants right over each grate. Turn heat to high. Use tongs to turn as each side is charred. After each eggplant is completely charred, place into a colander over a bowl; allow to cool. Discard any liquid.

Scoop the pumpkin from the rind; discard rind. On your cutting board, mash pumpkin with a fork; place into a bowl.

Remove and discard the charred skin of the eggplant. Mash the flesh on the cutting board, chopping and scraping it with the side of your knife. Add it to the pumpkin. Sprinkle in the smoked paprika, sweet paprika, salt, cumin, cayenne, and preserved lemon. In a food processor fitted with the metal "S" blade, pulse the jalapeño and garlic. Add to mixture. Mix well to distribute spices.

To serve, spoon over couscous.

MELANZANE di *scarponcino*

One of my favorite spots on the Amalfi coast is the charming, serene coastal town of Sorrento. It is a wonderful place to stroll; the town straddles the cliffs that overlook the water toward Naples and Mt. Vesuvius. It was there that I learned this recipe for this dish, a pride of that Campania region. It is eggplant filled with all bright Italian ingredients. Scarponcino is Italian for "shoes." The traditional preparation calls for splitting the eggplant lengthwise to make 2 halves that look like children's shoes. As a side dish, I like the size of the rounds better.

 YIELDS **6-8 SERVINGS**

peanut *or* **canola oil**

extra-virgin olive oil

1-2 medium purple eggplants, *sliced into ¾-inch slices*

salt

3 cloves fresh garlic, *minced*

⅓ cup salt capers *or* **capers**

½ cup green olives, *pitted and roughly chopped*

½ cup Kalamata olives, *drained, pitted, roughly chopped*

12 medium-large cherry tomatoes, *chopped*

5 leaves fresh basil, *chopped*

1 cup warm marinara sauce

dried oregano

Pour equal amounts of peanut oil and olive oil into a large skillet to come up ½ inch on the pan. Heat over medium heat until very hot but not smoking. Panfry the eggplant slices for 2-3 minutes per side, until golden brown. Drain on paper towels. Season the eggplants with a small sprinkling of salt.

If using salt capers, they need to be soaked in water to remove the salt. If using regular capers, rinse them very well to remove the acidic taste. In a large skillet, heat 2 tablespoons olive oil. Add the garlic; cook for 1 minute until fragrant, do not allow to brown. Add the capers, green olives, and Kalamata olives. Sauté for 5 minutes. Add the tomatoes; cook for 1 minute. Sprinkle in the fresh basil; add marinara sauce. Season with oregano to taste.

Remove the mixture from heat; spread over each of the eggplant slices. Can be made in advance and reheated.

harissa *maple* ROASTED PARSNIPS

Hey, sriracha, say hello to the newest member at the hot sauce party! Harissa is a North African paste, with ingredients that vary between countries and regions. It is available online and in some markets, and it's great on eggs and meats, in soups, as a cracker dip, and so much more. While this recipe is not traditional, as it does not include the standard dried smoked chilies, you get the reminiscent heat from the cayenne.

YIELDS **4-6 SERVINGS**

10 small-medium parsnips, *peeled*

¼ cup extra-virgin olive oil

3 tablespoons real maple syrup *(not pancake syrup)*

1 tablespoon tomato paste

1 tablespoon fresh lemon juice

1 clove fresh garlic, minced

1½ teaspoons cumin

½ teaspoon cayenne pepper

¼ teaspoon ground coriander

¼ teaspoon salt

Preheat the oven to 375°F. Line 2 baking sheets or jellyroll pans with parchment paper. Set aside.

Cut each parsnip in half widthwise, then cut each half into quarters or halves, depending on how thick, to make evenly sized 2-3-inch sticks.

In a medium bowl, combine olive oil, maple syrup, tomato paste, lemon juice, garlic, cumin, cayenne, coriander, and salt. Using gloved hands, add the parsnips; toss to coat.

Transfer to prepared baking sheets, leaving room between parsnips. Roast, uncovered, for 35 minutes, rotating the pans halfway through the cooking time. Immediately remove from the parchment so the drippings on the paper don't harden.

balsamic glazed **ONIONS**

"Cipolline Agro Dolce," or sweet and sour onions, are a traditional Roman dish. The gorgeous glazed onions are wonderful as a side for meat, veal, or chicken. Christopher Ranch makes and sells bags of peeled Cipollini onions, with a hechsher, at stores like Fairway. That's a great time-saver. If you cannot find the bags of peeled Cipollini onions, bring a large pot of salted water to a boil. Drop in the Cipollini; cook until blanched, about 3 minutes. Drain and cool under cold running water. Make a shallow slit down the side of each onion and slip off the skin.

 YIELDS **6-8 SERVINGS**

2 tablespoons extra-virgin olive oil

2 shallots, *peeled and minced*

2 cloves garlic, *minced*

½ teaspoon fine sea salt

¼ teaspoon freshly ground black pepper

1 pound *(30-35)* peeled Cipollini *or* pearl onions

½ cup balsamic vinegar

½ cup red wine, *such as Cabernet Sauvignon*

1 tablespoon honey

1 tablespoon tomato paste

1 dried bay leaf

In a large pot, heat the oil over medium heat. Add the shallots, garlic, salt, and pepper. Sauté for 3 minutes, until fragrant. Add the onions. Sauté for 7-8 minutes, until they just begin to color.

Add the vinegar, wine, honey, tomato paste, and bay leaf. Bring to a boil. Reduce heat; simmer for 10 minutes, until the sauce is concentrated and thickened and the onions are tender.

chili DELICATA SQUASH
with *blueberry honey*

Meet my favorite squash. I greet it in the market each fall like a long-lost friend. Delicata squash is a delicate beauty with gorgeous striped skin that is thin and pretty. Easy to carry, easy to cut, it needs no fancy preparation to shine. The flesh is creamy and becomes deliciously caramelized when roasted.

To avoid concentrating it in one area, sprinkle the chili powder from shoulder height.

Pure blueberry honey is the result of bees gathering nectar from the blueberry bush, and so the taste is reminiscent of that light, floral flavor. It is light amber in color, so if you can't find blueberry honey, use another mild honey.

(P) YIELDS **6-8 SERVINGS**

2-3 medium *(1½-2 pounds)* **Delicata squash**

3-4 tablespoons extra-virgin olive oil

1-2 teaspoons chili powder

2-3 tablespoons blueberry honey *or* **other mild honey**

Preheat the oven to 400°F. Line 2-3 baking sheets or jellyroll pans with parchment paper.

Slice off the ends of the squash. Slice squash crosswise into ½-inch rings. Use a melon baller or spoon to scrape out and discard the seeds. Spread the squash rings in a single layer on prepared sheets.

Drizzle with the olive oil; rub in to coat each squash ring on both sides. Lightly sprinkle evenly with the chili powder; lightly drizzle with honey.

Roast, uncovered, for 35-40 minutes.

chestnut *tomato* QUINOA

If the sun-dried tomatoes you have are very dry, rehydrate them in hot water for 5 minutes before pulsing them in the food processor. To present as in the photo, coat an oval measuring cup or silicone mold with nonstick cooking spray. Pack with the quinoa; unmold onto serving platter.

 YIELDS **8-10 SERVINGS**

10 packaged sundried tomato halves, *not packed in oil*

1 *(3.5-ounce)* **bag roasted and shelled whole chestnuts**

2 tablespoons oregano

1 tablespoon dried parsley

2 cups quinoa *if not pre-rinsed, rinse in a fine mesh strainer (see page 108)*

4½ cups water

¼ teaspoon fine sea salt

In the bowl of a food processor fitted with the metal "S" blade, pulse the tomatoes, chestnuts, oregano, and parsley until chopped; don't over-process or it will become a paste.

Place the quinoa and the chestnut mixture into a medium pot. Add water and salt. Bring to a boil; reduce heat to a simmer and allow the quinoa to bubble and cook for 15-18 minutes, or until it has absorbed all the liquid. The outer germ layer will separate and the grains will look shiny. Transfer to serving bowl.

silan shaved BRUSSELS SPROUTS

Many markets sell shredded Brussels sprouts. If yours doesn't or for a more economical way, it is simple to slice the Brussels sprouts using the slicing blade on a food processor; just cut off the root end and toss them down the feeding tube. A hand-held mandolin works fine as well. Since Brussels sprouts are part of the cabbage family, shredded green cabbage works fine here as well.

 YIELDS **4-6 SERVINGS**

1½ tablespoons dark brown sugar

2 teaspoons garlic powder

1 teaspoon chili powder

1 teaspoon coarse sea salt *or* kosher salt

¼ teaspoon cayenne pepper

2 tablespoons canola oil

2 pounds *(about 30)* Brussels sprouts, *shaved or shredded*

10 Brussels sprouts, *roots trimmed, halved*

1 tablespoon silan *(date syrup)*

In a small bowl, stir together the brown sugar, garlic powder, chili powder, salt, and cayenne.

Heat the oil in a large (14-inch) skillet or frying pan. (If you don't have a very large frying pan, divide the Brussels sprouts between 2 pans.) Add the shredded and the halved Brussels sprouts. Sprinkle on the spice mixture.

Cook sprouts, tossing them from time to time, allowing them to become shiny and almost burnt, 5-6 minutes. Drizzle in the silan. Cook for 1 minute longer.

Transfer to serving bowl.

sweet potato WONTONS
with teriyaki dipping sauce

This is a great way to use up leftover baked sweet potatoes.

 YIELDS **32-36 WONTONS**

SWEET POTATO WONTONS

2 medium sweet potatoes

3 tablespoons crushed pineapple, *drained well, reserve juice*

1 package wonton wrappers

canola oil

DIPPING SAUCE

¼ cup pineapple juice, *from the canned pineapple*

⅓ cup low-sodium soy sauce

2 tablespoons hoisin sauce

2 tablespoons ketchup

1 tablespoon dark brown sugar

juice of ½ lime

Preheat the oven to 400°F. Double wrap each sweet potato in aluminum foil. Place on a baking sheet to catch any drips. Roast for 45-60 minutes, until the potatoes are soft.

When the potatoes are cool enough to handle, peel them; mash the sweet potato flesh on your cutting board with the tines of a fork. Stir and mash in the crushed pineapple. Transfer to a bowl. Set aside.

Prepare the dipping sauce: Over medium heat, in a small pot, combine the pineapple juice, soy sauce, hoisin sauce, ketchup, brown sugar, and lime juice. Bring to a simmer. Cook for 3-4 minutes. Remove from heat. Set aside.

Heat 3-4 inches canola oil in a 6-8-quart pot.

Meanwhile, spread 12 wonton wrappers over your work surface. Place 1 rounded teaspoon of the sweet potato filling into the center of each wrapper. Don't overfill or they will leak. Run a wet finger around the perimeter of each wrapper. Fold over into a triangle, pressing to seal, pushing out any air. Repeat twice more, using 12 wrappers each time. The number you make will vary based on the size of your sweet potatoes. I average 32-36 wontons per batch.

When the oil reaches 350-375°F, fry the wontons, 5-6 at a time; do not crowd the pot. Use tongs to remove to a paper towel-lined platter. Repeat until all the wontons are fried. Serve with the dipping sauce.

CAULIFLOWER *milanese*

Milanese is a classic Italian preparation that is traditionally used for veal cutlets that are pounded thin, breaded, and fried. I loved the idea of using it for cauliflower and swapping in pickles for the capers that would traditionally be in the sauce. The cornmeal gives it a nice crunch.

 YIELDS **4-6 SERVINGS**

CAULIFLOWER

2 large eggs

2 tablespoons Dijon mustard

1 teaspoon lemon juice

¾ teaspoon fine sea salt

½ teaspoon cayenne pepper

½ cup seasoned dry breadcrumbs

½ cup fine yellow cornmeal

1½ teaspoons dried parsley

1 teaspoon kosher *or* coarse salt

1½ pounds *(1 large head)* **cauliflower florets**

nonstick cooking spray

DIPPING SAUCE

⅓ cup mayonnaise

2 tablespoons spicy brown mustard

½ sour pickle, *minced*

1 tablespoon pickle juice, *from any kind of pickle*

½ teaspoon Worcestershire sauce

¼ teaspoon ground black pepper

¼ teaspoon paprika

¼ teaspoon garlic powder

Preheat the oven to 400°F. Line 1-2 baking sheets or jellyroll pans with parchment paper. Set aside.

In a shallow bowl, whisk the eggs, Dijon mustard, lemon juice, fine sea salt, and cayenne.

Place the breadcrumbs, cornmeal, parsley, and kosher salt into a gallon-sized heavy-duty ziplock bag.

Dip the cauliflower, 1 handful at a time, into the egg mixture, coating well. Then transfer the cauliflower into the ziplock bag. Shake to coat completely. Arrange in a single layer on prepared pan. Continue until all the cauliflower is breaded. Do not crowd the pan; use a second one if needed. Coat heavily with cooking spray on all exposed surfaces; this will help with crisping.

Roast, uncovered, for 35 minutes. After 20 minutes, spray the cauliflower again with cooking spray if it looks dry.

Meanwhile, prepare the dipping sauce: In a medium bowl, whisk together the mayonnaise, spicy brown mustard, minced pickle, pickle juice, Worcestershire sauce, pepper, paprika, and garlic powder.

Serve the cauliflower with the dipping sauce.

ancie's KUGEL

I will always treasure the days back a few years ago, when my friend Ancie Cohenson (a"h) came to live with my family for a short while. An octogenarian Holocaust survivor, she had endured many hardships but always had a smile and a kind word. My kids adored her. As a thank-you for hosting her, she had a pre-Shabbos ritual of making us a skillet potato kugel that never even made it till candle-lighting. Her kugel was slowly cooked in a frying pan over the fire. The crust becomes a crisp, deep brown and encases a soft, velvety, white interior, almost like a giant creamy latka. The grater pictured and mentioned in the recipe is what she used, and following the ritual reminds me of her, so I don't deviate. However, I am sure a food processor would work fine, too.

 YIELDS **6 SERVINGS**

3 russet potatoes, *peeled*

½ medium onion, *peeled*

3 large eggs, *lightly beaten*

¼ cup matzoh meal

1 teaspoon kosher salt

½ teaspoon freshly ground black pepper

¾ cup canola oil

Peel and rinse the potatoes. Using a Kuchenprofi Potato Grater/Shredder or a safety grater (see photo), grate 2 potatoes into a bowl. Grate the onion half and then the third potato. Add the eggs, matzoh meal, salt, and pepper. Stir well to combine. Set aside.

In a heavy 10-inch skillet (a well-seasoned cast-iron skillet is perfect, but a heavy nonstick pan is fine) over medium heat, heat the oil for a full 2-3 minutes until hot. Carefully add potato mixture, spreading it into an even layer with the back of a wooden spoon. Scoop up some oil from the sides to spread over the top.

Reduce the heat to low or medium-low; you should see and hear very gentle sizzling around the outside of the kugel, but not more than that or it will burn during the long cooking time. Cook for 5 minutes, uncovered, then cover the pan and cook for 30 minutes.

Uncover; cook to dry the kugel a bit, 5 minutes. Using a thin spatula to get under the kugel to loosen it, carefully slide the kugel out onto a plate. Cover kugel with a second plate; flip the kugel. If the skillet is dry, add 1 tablespoon of oil. Carefully slide the kugel back into the skillet, crust-side up. Cook, uncovered until well browned on the second side, 25-30 minutes.

Slide the kugel onto a platter or plate. Cut into wedges; serve hot.

freekah PILAF

Move over, quinoa: there's a new ancient grain in town and it's called freekah! Legend has it that around 2,000 years ago in the Middle East, a field of young green wheat was set on fire during an attack. When local villagers returned to the scene, they discovered that their crop was actually not ruined; when they rubbed away the charred outer coating, the inner grain was still edible, with a lightly smoked flavor — and freekah was born. I love that it is a firm, slightly chewy grain, with a distinct flavor that's earthy and nutty. It is loaded with fiber and protein to boot. When I smell it raw, it smells grassy like bird seed, but once it's cooked, it is divine and is a blank canvas for any add-in ingredients for salads, tabbouleh, or grain recipes.

 YIELDS 8-10 SERVINGS

4 tablespoons canola oil, *divided*

1 medium onion, *peeled, cut into ¼-inch dice*

1 clove fresh garlic, *minced*

14 ounces *(2½ cups)* **freekah**

5 cups water

1 teaspoon fine sea salt, *divided*

½ cup pine nuts

1 cup sliced black olives

¼ cup golden raisins

1 cup curly parsley, *chopped*

¼ cup extra-virgin olive oil

zest and juice of ½ navel orange

Preheat the oven to 375°F.

Heat 3 tablespoons canola oil in a medium, ovenproof pot that has a lid. Add the onion; cook over medium heat until shiny and translucent, 5-6 minutes. Do not allow it to brown. Add the garlic; cook for 1 minute. Add the freekah; toast, mixing it well with the onion for 4-5 minutes. It will be fragrant. Add water and ½ teaspoon salt. Bring to a boil, then cover the pot and transfer to the oven for 20 minutes.

Place the pine nuts and remaining tablespoon canola oil into a small pot. Toast over medium heat, shaking the nuts the whole time until golden and fragrant, about 3 minutes. They may be darker in some spots but don't allow them to burn.

When the freekah is done, remove the lid; allow to cool for a few minutes. Stir in the olives, raisins, parsley, pine nuts, olive oil, orange zest, orange juice, and remaining ½ teaspoon salt. Transfer to serving dish.

sweet potato coconut **CASSEROLE**

This one is all about home. Nothing says "holiday table" to me more than a sweet potato casserole. Current thinking places coconut oil as the king of the oils, bringing with it lots of health benefits. The coconut flavors in this recipe are subtle, but really add a nice background note, making this a bit different from traditional sweet potato casseroles.

 OR YIELDS **10-12 SERVINGS**

4½ pounds *(about 8 medium)* **sweet potatoes**

½ cup dark brown sugar

6 tablespoons coconut oil, margarine, or butter, *softened*

¼ cup coconut milk

2 large eggs

1 teaspoon pure vanilla extract

½ teaspoon cinnamon

¼ teaspoon fine sea salt

1¼ cups cornflakes cereal

1 cup chopped walnuts

½ cup shredded coconut flakes, *sweetened or unsweetened*

1 tablespoon brown sugar

1 tablespoon coconut oil, *melted*

1 *(8-ounce)* **bag marshmallows**

Preheat the oven to 400°F. Line a jellyroll pan with foil. Coat a 9 x 13-inch oven-to-table casserole dish with nonstick cooking spray. Set aside.

Place sweet potatoes onto prepared jellyroll pan; bake for 1 hour, or until a knife easily pierces the flesh. Let stand until cool enough to handle. Slit the skins lengthwise and, using 2 paper towels to protect your hands, peel the potatoes. Place flesh into the bowl of a stand mixer and mash it with the back of a spoon or potato masher. Reduce oven temperature to 350°F.

In the bowl of the stand mixer fitted with the paddle attachment, mix mashed sweet potatoes, brown sugar, coconut oil, coconut milk, eggs, vanilla, cinnamon, and salt. Beat until smooth. Spoon potato mixture into prepared casserole dish.

Place the cornflakes into a medium bowl. Crush them by hand, leaving some texture — do not crush too fine. Add the walnuts, coconut, brown sugar, and melted coconut oil. Sprinkle over casserole in diagonal rows, leaving 1 inch between each row.

Bake for 30 minutes. Remove from oven. Arrange marshmallows side-by-side, alternating with the rows of cornflake mixture; bake 10 minutes. Serve hot.

roasted VEGETABLE *crisps*

This tempting side dish also doubles as a snack with any sort of dip.

 YIELDS **4-6 SERVINGS**

1 large zucchini, *ends trimmed, not peeled*

1 large sweet potato, *ends trimmed, not peeled*

1 Yukon Gold potato, *ends trimmed, not peeled*

3 tablespoons all-purpose flour

1 tablespoon garlic powder

1 tablespoon dried oregano

1 teaspoon dried parsley

½ teaspoon kosher *or* **coarse sea salt**

¼ teaspoon cayenne pepper

olive oil-flavored nonstick cooking spray

Preheat the oven to 350°F. Line 2 large baking sheets or jellyroll pans with parchment paper.

Using a sharp knife or a hand-held mandolin, thinly slice the vegetables into ¼-inch-thick slices; don't make them thinner or the chips will burn.

Place sliced vegetables between 2 sheets of paper towels; press to absorb some of the liquid. Press extra hard on the zucchini. Transfer all to a large mixing bowl.

In a small bowl, stir together the flour, garlic powder, oregano, parsley, salt, and cayenne. Sprinkle over the vegetables; toss to coat every slice well on both sides. Spread in even layers onto prepared pans; the vegetables can be close to each other since they shrink, just try not to overlap them. Coat generously with cooking spray. Turn each over and spray the other side.

Bake, uncovered, for 40 minutes, checking after 30 minutes to make sure they are crisp and golden but not burning; they may need a few more minutes or you may have to remove the more done pieces. Turn off the oven; leave the trays in the oven and allow to crisp until the oven has cooled down completely.

MUJADARA

Part of planning the Foodie Tour in Israel is to find fun, active, culinary experiences for the guests. We came across a great one that I recommend if you have a family or group of friends in Jerusalem. The company is called Te'amim. They have an industrial kitchen in the old covered shuk attached to Machane Yehuda. They break the group into teams and together the teams create a full meal, featuring traditional Israeli-Arabic dishes. The friendly competition for "best dish" keeps things lively, and the payoff is there for everyone as you all enjoy a feast from the Middle East!

 YIELDS **12 SERVINGS**

LENTILS

1 cup brown *or* **Puy lentils;** *I like Puy lentils*

4 teaspoons cumin, *divided*

water to cover

RICE

4 cups water

1 tablespoon extra-virgin olive oil

2 cups basmati *or* **jasmine rice**

1 cinnamon stick

2 dried bay leaves

½ teaspoon ground coriander

1 teaspoon fine sea salt, *divided*

¼ teaspoon black pepper

3 large onions, *peeled, halved, very thinly sliced*

¼ cup all-purpose flour

1 tablespoon turmeric

canola oil

Prepare the lentils: Place the lentils and 2 teaspoons cumin into a medium pot. Cover with 2 inches of water. Bring to a boil. Reduce heat; simmer for 20-30 minutes (brown lentils take longer than Puy lentils). Cook until the lentils are just soft. Do not allow them to overcook and become mushy. Drain and set aside.

Prepare the rice: Bring the 4 cups of water to a boil. Meanwhile, heat the tablespoon of olive oil in a large pot that has a tight lid. Add rice, cinnamon stick, bay leaves, coriander, ½ teaspoon salt, and pepper. Stir well to coat the rice. Add the boiling water. Seal the pot with aluminum foil and then the lid. Reduce heat to a simmer; cook for 18-20 minutes. Make sure no steam is escaping. Turn off heat; allow rice to rest, covered, for 10 minutes. Fluff with a fork. Discard bay leaves and cinnamon stick. Stir in the drained lentils.

Meanwhile, heat 2 inches of canola oil in a pot or high-sided skillet. Place the onions into a medium bowl. Toss with flour and turmeric, coating onion slices well. Test the oil with a tiny bit of flour; when hot enough, the oil should bubble around flour. Add half the onions; fry for 7 minutes, or until golden. Remove with a slotted spoon. Repeat with remaining onions.

Stir half the onions into the rice mixture. Sprinkle the remaining ½ teaspoon salt on the remaining onions and pile them on the rice to garnish.

Fruit market, Mexico

Halvah
Sarona Market,
Tel Aviv, Israel

Verona, Italy

Ruggies at the Shuk
Jerusalem, Israel

Date farm, Israel

SPECIALITA' ✡ DOLCI EBRAICI ✡ SI ACCETTANO ORDINAZIONI

Impade €1,50 al pezzo

Bakery display, Venice, Italy

Desserts

LEMON *tiramisu*

Volcanic soil, perfect temperature, and just the right amount of rain result in spectacular and sweet lemons that grow all along the Amalfi Coast. Visit Sorrento and you can find Italy's sunshine in a bottle in the form of Limoncello. A time-honored tradition, Limoncello is a liquor made using Amalfi Coast lemons and sold in exquisite bottles all throughout Sorrento. Reach out to the local rabbinic authority if you are visiting, because it is possible to find it kosher.

This recipe is an ode to those lemons. It is also lovely as an individual dessert served in ramekins. After soaking the ladyfingers in Limoncello, cut with a cookie cutter that just fits into your selected ramekin. Use a thin spatula to move the ladyfingers to the ramekin. Then layer the curd and cream. Layer them thick and you will need only one layer of each. If the alcohol is too strong or the recipe is for children, water it down or use lemonade.

 OR ⓟ   YIELDS **9 SERVINGS**

6 tablespoons unsalted butter *or* **margarine,** *at room temperature*

1 cup sugar *plus* **2 tablespoons,** *divided*

2 large eggs *plus* **2 egg yolks**

⅔ cup lemon juice *(from 4-5 lemons)*

2 teaspoons lemon zest, *divided*

2 cups heavy whipping cream *or* **nondairy whipped topping**

2 *(3-ounce)* **packages soft sponge** *or* **hard ladyfingers** *(24 per package)*

Limoncello, *such as Binyamina brand*

Line a plastic or glass rectangular or square container with plastic wrap, leaving enough overhang to completely enclose the lemon curd. Set aside.

In a stand mixer fitted with the paddle attachment, beat the butter and 1 cup sugar for 2 minutes. Slowly add the eggs and yolks, beating for 1 minute. With the machine running, slowly pour in the lemon juice; it is okay if it doesn't look smooth. Transfer to a pot.

Cook the lemon mixture over low heat for 15 minutes, whisking gently almost the whole time. It will thicken, but don't allow it to boil or get brown on the bottom of the pot; gentle bubbles are okay. The lemon curd will become smooth, thicker, and darker in color. Stir in 1 teaspoon lemon zest. Pour the lemon curd into the prepared container, folding the sides of the plastic wrap to cover curd in order to keep a skin from forming. Seal the container; place in refrigerator to cool completely.

When lemon curd is cold, whip the whipping cream to firm peaks.

Place the ladyfingers on your cutting board; drizzle lightly with the Limoncello.

Place a layer of ladyfingers into a glass or ceramic pan. Spread a thin layer of the lemon curd over the ladyfingers. Top with a layer of cream. Repeat twice more.

Place remaining teaspoon lemon zest and remaining 2 tablespoons sugar into a medium bowl. Rub sugar and zest together between your palms to combine. Sprinkle over tiramisu. You can substitute culinary lavender rubbed together with sugar for a similar garnish (see photo).

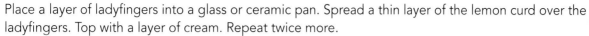

almond **CHOCOLATE CHIP** *sticks*

The recipe for chocolate chip sticks in the Kosher Palette *cookbook became a standard in thousands of homes. Somehow, they came out differently for all bakers, with my friend Marisa's being my favorite. This year for Passover, I tinkered with the recipe to use it on the holiday and my family declared that the cookies were so great, I "ended the suffering of the Jews." I was so pleased to cut out white flour, that I have started making them this way all year round. Gluten free people, rejoice! These cookies get a bit softer overnight. If you don't like that texture, store them in the freezer.*

 YIELDS **20-25 COOKIES**

½ cup canola *or* vegetable oil

½ cup sugar

½ cup firmly packed dark brown sugar

1 large egg, *lightly beaten*

1 teaspoon pure vanilla extract

1 cup *plus* 2 tablespoons (5-ounces) quinoa flour

¼ cup plus 2 tablespoons (2-ounces) finely ground almond flour

2 tablespoons potato starch

1 teaspoon baking soda

½ teaspoon salt

½ cup good-quality chocolate chips

Preheat the oven to 350°F. Line a large cookie sheet with parchment paper. Set aside.

In the bowl of a stand mixer fitted with the paddle attachment, combine the oil, sugar, and brown sugar. Mix well. Stir in the egg and vanilla.

In a medium bowl, combine the quinoa flour, almond flour, potato starch, baking soda, and salt. Stir into the egg mixture. Blend well. Mix in the chocolate chips.

Divide the dough in half. Place on the prepared sheet. Form the dough into 2 (3 x 12-inch) logs. Wet your hands if needed to manipulate the dough.

Bake for 22 minutes or until golden brown. Cool for 10 minutes; cut while slightly warm into thin sticks.

Store in an airtight container.

BANANA, *date, and pecan* cake

A fascinating stop on my Israel Foodie Tour one year was to the Dan Gourmet Fine Culinary Arts Cooking Center, where we took a professional patisserie class. All the desserts were complicated, multistep, and way above our skill level, but with the assistance of a great teacher, we had incredibly exciting results. This cake, which was an element of a grander dessert, was a crowd favorite on its own, as it is not too sweet; perfect with a cup of tea or coffee after a meal.

 OR Ⓟ   YIELDS **8 SERVINGS**

2 large eggs

⅓ cup sugar

½ cup canola oil

1 cup all-purpose flour

½ teaspoon cinnamon

¼ teaspoon nutmeg

1 teaspoon baking soda

1 teaspoon baking powder

1 ripe medium-large banana, *cut into ½-inch dice*

⅔ cup chopped pecans

¼ cup good-quality chocolate chips

6 dates, *pitted, halved, and sliced*

3 ounces good quality semisweet chocolate, *finely chopped*

¼ cup heavy cream *or* nondairy whipped topping

Preheat the oven to 350°F. Line an 11 x 7-inch brownie pan with parchment paper. Coat with nonstick cooking spray. Set aside.

In the bowl of a stand mixer fitted with the paddle attachment, beat the eggs and the sugar at high speed, for a full 5 minutes, until thick ribbons form.

Reduce mixer speed; slowly pour in the oil.

In a medium bowl, stir together flour, cinnamon, nutmeg, baking soda, and baking powder. Gradually add to mixer bowl; beat at low speed until well blended.

Add banana, pecans, chocolate chips, and dates. Mix until well blended.

Pour into prepared pan; bake for 20-22 minutes, until a toothpick inserted in center comes out dry or with moist crumbs.

Place into freezer for 15 minutes.

Using the parchment paper, lift the cake out to a cutting board. Cut in half lengthwise. Cut each half into 16 slices.

Place the chocolate into a bowl. Heat the cream in the microwave or in a small pot. Pour over the chocolate; stir until chocolate has melted. Drizzle in a zig-zag fashion over the cake slices.

nutella *peanut butter* CHEESECAKE

Gianduja, a specialty of Turin, Italy is a chocolate-hazelnut confection. Its commercial cousin, Nutella, has taken this country and my family's heart by storm. Shamelessly rich and indulgent, there is no better combination for a cheesecake than Nutella and peanut butter.

 YIELDS **12 SERVINGS**

NUTELLA CRUST

1 cup Nutella

1 tablespoon dark brown sugar

1 large egg

½ cup *plus* 1 tablespoon all-purpose flour

¼ teaspoon Maldon salt, coarse sea salt, *or* kosher salt

CHEESECAKE FILLING

4 *(8-ounce)* blocks cream cheese, *at room temperature*

1 cup sugar

1 teaspoon pure vanilla extract

4 large eggs

½ cup creamy peanut butter

½ cup Nutella

NUTELLA GLAZE

½ cup Nutella

Preheat the oven to 325°F. Lightly coat a 9-inch springform pan with nonstick cooking spray, set aside.

Prepare the crust: In the bowl of a stand mixer fitted with the paddle attachment, beat 1 cup Nutella, brown sugar, egg, flour, and salt together for 1-2 minutes to form a smooth dough. Press dough into the bottom of prepared pan. Bake for 8 minutes. Set aside to cool.

Prepare the filling: In a clean mixing bowl, beat cream cheese and sugar together until smooth. Add in vanilla; add one egg at a time, mixing between each until just combined. Don't over-mix. Scrape down the sides and bottom of bowl during mixing.

Remove 2½ cups batter to a medium bowl. Set aside.

Add the peanut butter to the remaining batter. Beat until smooth. Pour peanut butter mixture over cookie base. Using a small offset spatula, smooth the batter.

No need to wash the bowl or beater. Pour the reserved batter back into the mixer bowl. Add ½ cup Nutella; beat until smooth. Pour over the peanut butter layer; use a small, clean offset spatula to smooth into an even layer.

Bake for 55-60 minutes, until center is almost set. Remove from oven and allow to cool.

Prepare the glaze: Microwave ½ cup Nutella for 30 seconds.

Spread glaze in an even layer over the center of the cake. Cover and refrigerate for at least 4 hours before serving. Make sure you cut all the way to the bottom of the cookie crust; a serrated knife will help.

CANNOLI sandwiches

Cannoli are the Sicilian gift to the dessert table. This recipe, inspired by true cannoli, is foolproof for the non-bakers out there! Cannoli shells are a hassle to make from scratch and store-bought shells are never fresh. Using liberties that a cook can, I took out the best part — the cream — and made it a stand-alone star. This is a quick and easy dessert that can be made in advance.

 YIELDS **4 SERVINGS**

1 cup full-fat ricotta cheese, *drained*

4 ounces mascarpone cheese *or* **block cream cheese**

1 tablespoon heavy cream

1 cup confectioner's sugar

½ teaspoon vanilla extract

pizzelle *(or ice-cream sugar cones, for dipping)*

½ cup mini semisweet chocolate chips *and/or* **chopped raw pistachios**

In the bowl of a stand mixer fitted with the paddle attachment, beat the drained ricotta, mascarpone, cream, sugar, and vanilla until just smooth. Do not overbeat. Transfer to serving bowl. Allow to chill at least 4 hours.

Shortly before serving, to avoid soggy pizzelle, sandwich ½-inch of filling between 2 pizzelle. Place in freezer for 10 minutes; the cream should be tacky to the touch.

Roll the edges of half the sandwiches in mini chips and the other half in chopped pistachios, if using. Freeze for 15 minutes more.

Alternatively, serve the cannolli filling in a pretty bowl, garnished with mini chocolate chips and/or pistachio nuts. Serve with pizzelle or broken ice-cream cones to scoop like a dip.

SBRISOLONA

Sbrisolona is a rustic specialty of Mantova, Italy, right outside of Verona, where I worked on a culinary tour in July 2015. Like so much traditional Italian food, sbrisolona was created with what were known as "poor" and "local" ingredients. In this case, it is cornmeal, which is added to the white flour, as it was cheaper and more easily available.

Sbrisolona is Italian for "crumbly." It is more of a giant cookie than a cake and, in fact, in Italy, it is broken with your hands or a wooden spoon right at the table, with everyone getting some chunks and pieces. Although it's not traditional, I like serving this with a warm blueberry sauce (see recipe on facing page), sort of like a deconstructed blueberry crisp.

 D OR **P**   YIELDS **8-10 SERVINGS**

2 large egg yolks

2 teaspoons pure vanilla extract

1 teaspoon almond extract

zest of 1 lemon *or* ½ orange

1½ cups *(7 ounces)* blanched slivered *or* sliced almonds

1 cup *(6 ounces)* fine *or* medium ground yellow cornmeal

1 cup sugar

1 cup *plus* 2 tablespoons all-purpose flour

1 cup *(2 sticks)* butter *or* margarine, *at room temperature*

22 whole raw almonds, *with skin*

Preheat the oven to 350°F. Coat a 9- or 10-inch spring-form pan with nonstick cooking spray; line with parchment paper. Set aside.

In a small bowl, whisk the egg yolks, vanilla extract, almond extract, and lemon zest. Set aside.

In a food processor fitted with the metal "S" blade, pulse the slivered almonds until roughly chopped; do not grind them to a powder.

Transfer almonds to a large mixing bowl. Add cornmeal, sugar, and flour. Mix. Tear the butter into small pieces as you add it to the bowl. Crumble and toss the mixture with your fingers or a pastry blender until it resembles coarse crumbs, like streusel or big coffee-cake crumbs. Pour in the egg yolk mixture; pinch it in as well, being careful to not over-mix. Leave large crumbs.

Transfer to prepared pan. Loosely press the crumbs around the edges and top; don't compress the crumbs, leave it bumpy. Scatter on the whole raw almonds. Bake 40 minutes or until a deep golden brown.

Remove from oven and allow to cool for 15 minutes. Unmold it right on a cutting board; use a wooden spoon to break off servings or use your hands to break off chunks. Serve with blueberry sauce if desired.

BLUEBERRY *Sauce*

In a small saucepan, combine 1 cup (6 ounces) fresh or frozen blueberries, ¼ cup water, ½ cup orange juice, and ⅓ cup sugar. Bring to a boil. In a small bowl, mix 1 tablespoon cornstarch with 3 tablespoons cold water. Add to the pot; return mixture to a simmer until it thickens, about 3 minutes. Transfer to bowl. Allow to cool; serve with the Sbrisolona.

french NAPOLEONS

Although Napoleons are traditionally French, and I did see them all over pastry shop windows in France, it was not until I had a personal motive that I decided to tackle them. For my sister Karen's 50th birthday, I brought the restaurant to her. Together we prepared a spectacular dinner in her happiest of places — her newly designed kitchen — and enjoyed it al fresco with our husbands on a glorious summer night. I am happy to share that although there are multiple steps, they are actually all quite simple. This is a great dessert to add to your repertoire. I experimented multiple times to get the recipe right. It is worlds better when you use dairy puff pastry made with butter in lieu of parve pastry made with shortening. The brand I love is Dufours, which you can get at Whole Foods and upscale specialty food stores.

 YIELDS **8 SERVINGS**

PASTRY
2 *(14-17.3 ounce)* **packages puff pastry,** *thawed*
2 tablespoons butter, *melted*

VANILLA CUSTARD
6 large egg yolks
3 tablespoons all-purpose flour
3 tablespoons cornstarch
1½ cups whole milk
1½ cups heavy cream
1 vanilla bean
¾ cup sugar
1 tablespoon pure vanilla extract
½ teaspoon salt

GLAZES
2 ounces good-quality milk chocolate
2 cups confectioner's sugar
4 teaspoons corn syrup
4-6 tablespoons milk, *plus more as needed*

Prepare the vanilla custard: Set a medium bowl into a larger bowl filled with ice. Don't let the ice come up too far up on the outside of the medium bowl. Set a fine-mesh strainer over the medium bowl. Set aside.

In another medium bowl, whisk together egg yolks, flour, and cornstarch until well-combined. Set aside.

Pour milk and cream into a medium pot. Using the tip of a paring knife, place the vanilla bean on your cutting board; split the vanilla bean lengthwise. Scrape the seeds from the pod; add them to the pot along with the pod. Add the sugar, vanilla, and salt; simmer over medium-low heat. Slowly add heated milk mixture to the egg yolks, half-cup at a time, whisking constantly to ensure the egg yolks do not curdle. Once the milk mixture has been completely incorporated into the egg mixture, return the mixture to the pot. Discard the vanilla bean pod. Cook over medium heat, whisking constantly, for an additional 2-3 minutes, or until mixture is thick and bubbly. Dip a wooden spoon into the mixture. The custard is thickened enough when you run a finger across the mixture on the back of the spoon and a path remains.

Pour the custard through the prepared fine-mesh strainer into the bowl set on ice. Cover the bowl with plastic wrap, letting the wrap touch the surface so a skin doesn't form on the custard, or transfer custard to a heavy-duty pastry bag. Refrigerate for 2 hours, or up to 4 days.

Prepare the puff pastry: Preheat the oven to 375°F. Line two large cookie sheets or jellyroll pans with parchment paper. Place pastry dough onto a lightly floured surface; roll each sheet out to ⅛-inch thickness, keeping rectangular shape. Cut each sheet into 12 even rectangles, for a total of 24. Transfer to prepared pans; poke all over with a fork and brush with melted butter. Bake until golden brown and flaky, 12-14 minutes. Remove from oven; allow to cool completely.

Prepare the glazes: Prepare a cookie cooling rack. Melt the chocolate in a microwave-safe bowl using 30-second increments, stirring after each. Transfer to a ziplock bag or small pastry bag. Set aside.

In another medium bowl, whisk together confectioner's sugar and corn syrup. Add milk, 1 tablespoon at a time, until you reach a consistency that is pourable but still thick. Working individually, dip one flat surface of 8 of the puff pastry rectangles into the glaze; place onto the cookie cooling rack to set. Spread with an offset spatula if needed. Cut the tip off the bag of chocolate. Drizzle two thin lines of chocolate lengthwise over the icing. Drag a toothpick across perpendicular to the chocolate in alternating directions to make the classic Napoleon design.

To assemble, place a piece of plain baked puff pastry on a plate. Press it down to compact slightly. Top with a layer of custard. Compress a second piece of puff pastry and lay it over the custard. Top with a second layer of custard. Add a glazed puff pastry to the top. Repeat with remaining components.

Keep refrigerated in an airtight container for up to 3 days.

ilene's **OATMEAL** *cookies*

An invitation to Ilene and Steve Sheris's home always means a good time. They are fun, open-handed hosts who love to celebrate summer with friends at their pool in their yard. We love their happy spirit and great sense of humor. That would be enough to draw a crowd, but to seal the deal, Ilene makes sure to always have these oatmeal cookies on hand, as they are the group favorite. I had a blast with her in her kitchen, watching her make them … actually twice. We yakked so much the first time, we lost track of the time, and the batch had to be redone.

 YIELDS **24 COOKIES**

2¼ **cups old-fashioned oats** (not quick-cooking or instant), divided

1 **cup dark brown sugar**

½ **cup** *plus* 1 **tablespoon canola oil**

1 **large egg,** *beaten*

1 **tablespoon pure vanilla extract**

¼ **teaspoon fine sea salt**

Place 2 cups and 2 tablespoons of oats into a large mixing bowl. Add the brown sugar; roll between your palms and knead with your fingers to thoroughly distribute the sugar into the oats. Slowly drizzle the oil into the oats, mixing well, kneading with your fingers as you add it. Allow the mixture to stand for an hour; this allows the oats to soak up the oil and soften slightly.

Preheat the oven to 325°F. Line 2 cookie sheets or jellyroll pans with parchment paper. Set aside.

Make a well in the center of the oats. Pour in the egg, vanilla, and salt; mix well with a spoon until the mixture is pliable but holds together when pushed into a ball. Sprinkle in the remaining 2 tablespoons oats; mix well. Allow to stand for 5 minutes.

Using a large soup spoon, scoop out a full spoonful of batter, pressing against the side of the bowl for even shape and portions. Use a finger to slide the dough off the spoon onto the prepared sheets, leaving plenty of room for spreading (I bake 6 cookies to a sheet). Bake for 10-12 minutes, until the tops of the cookies are not sticky. They will be soft but should not be wet; they will firm up as they cool. You can switch the trays halfway through for even baking. Turn off the oven. Open the oven door to let cool air in for a few seconds. Close the door and let the cookies stay in the oven for 10 minutes. Remove from oven; after 5 minutes, transfer the cookies with a thin metal spatula to a cookie cooling rack until completely cool.

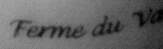

grilled PINEAPPLE

Let fresh fruit bring some sizzle to everyone's favorite part of the meal.

 YIELDS **6 SERVINGS**

½ cup **good-quality fruit preserves,** *any flavor*

¼ cup **honey**

1 tablespoon **balsamic vinegar**

pinch chili powder

1 **ripe pineapple,** *peeled, cut into 6 wedges*

olive oil-flavored nonstick cooking spray

In a small pot, combine preserves, honey, balsamic vinegar, and chili powder.

Meanwhile, heat a grill or a grill pan until very hot. Coat with cooking spray. Skewer the pineapple, using 2 skewers per wedge for support if they are very thin; place on the hot grill or pan. Brush with preserves mixture. Grill 3 minutes per side, brushing a few times on each side with preserves. Heat the remaining preserves over medium heat. Drizzle over the spears.

Serve hot.

almond BOBKA RING

You can make this show-stopping dessert in advance. Wrap it very well or place into an airtight container and freeze for up to 3 months. Thaw at room temperature; if re-warming in the oven, wrap well in foil to avoid burning.

 OR   YIELDS **8-10 SERVINGS**

DOUGH

⅔ **cup warm milk** *or* **soymilk**

2 **large eggs** *plus* 1 **egg yolk**

1 **stick** *(8 tablespoons)* **butter** *or* **margarine,** *cut into small cubes*

⅓ **cup warm** *(not hot)* **water**

⅓ **cup sugar**

1 **tablespoon active dry yeast** *or* **bread machine yeast**

4 **cups all-purpose** *or* **bread flour**

1½ **teaspoons fine sea salt**

FILLING

1 **cup dark brown sugar**

1 **tablespoon cinnamon**

4 **tablespoons melted butter** *or* **margarine**

2 **tablespoons cornstarch**

1 *(12-ounce)* **can almond filling** *(NOT almond paste), such as Luv N Bake's Schmear*

STREUSEL

½ **cup confectioner's sugar**

⅓ **cup all-purpose flour**

4 **tablespoons butter** *or* **margarine,** *cut into small cubes*

⅓ **cup sliced blanched almonds**

Prepare the dough: In the bowl of a stand mixer fitted with a dough hook, or by hand in a large bowl, combine the milk, eggs, yolk, ½ cup butter, water, sugar, and yeast. Mix for 1 minute. Add the flour and salt. Mix on medium until a smooth satiny dough forms, 5-6 minutes. If doing by hand, knead until the dough is satiny smooth, about 10 minutes. If using butter, you may need a few extra teaspoons of flour; add only one at a time until the dough is satiny. Allow the dough to rest for 10 minutes.

Meanwhile, prepare the filling: In a medium bowl, combine brown sugar, cinnamon, 4 tablespoons melted butter, and cornstarch. Stir until smooth. Reserve canned filling

Prepare the streusel: In a medium bowl, combine confectioner's sugar, ⅓ cup flour, 4 tablespoons butter, and almonds. Knead the mixture until it is evenly distributed and can be gathered into a ball. Set aside.

Coat a 10-inch tube pan with nonstick cooking spray.

On a lightly floured surface roll the dough into a 20 x 9-inch rectangle.

Spread canned almond filling over dough, leaving a ½-inch border. Sprinkle on the prepared filling mixture; use a small offset spatula to spread into an even layer. Starting from a long side, roll dough like a jellyroll; carefully seal the edges and ends. Cut the rolled dough in half lengthwise. Line the two halves side-by-side with cut sides up; loosely twist together, keeping the cut sides up. Transfer to prepared pan, forming the twist into a ring. Press the edges together to finish the ring.

Tear the streusel topping into small bits; toss over the top of the bobka. Cover; let rise in a warm place for 30-40 minutes, until doubled in size.

Preheat the oven to 350°F. Bake 35-40 minutes, or until golden brown. Cool in pan for 10 minutes; don't let it cool any longer or the cake will stick in the pan. Pull out the tube and then remove the bobka using a small offset spatula to release it from the bottom of the tube; use a plate to help support the cake as you flip it out. Turn the bobka right-side-up; cool completely on a wire rack. Serve completely cooled or re-warmed in the oven, wrapped in foil or unwrapped in the microwave.

melting CHOCOLATE meringues

This flourless cookie has no added fat from margarine, butter, or oil — it is sure to delight! But that is, of course, because it comes from one of my personal favorite authors and is adapted with permission from Alice Medrich's Chewy Gooey Crispy Crunchy. Nobody knows chocolate desserts better than Alice, and it is a treat to include one of her recipes here.

Warm egg whites whip better but are harder to separate from the yolks. If you don't have time to separate your eggs and let them sit for 30 minutes at room temperature, place them into a bowl of warm water for 5 minutes to get the chill off. Separate the eggs, then allow the whites to sit in the mixing bowl for another 10 minutes. Make sure there isn't any trace of yolk in the whites; if there is, they won't whip properly.

 YIELDS **20-24 COOKIES**

6 ounces best-quality bittersweet *or* **semisweet chocolate,** *finely chopped*

2 large egg whites, *at room temperature*

⅛ **teaspoon cream of tartar**

½ **teaspoon vanilla extract**

pinch of salt

¼ **cup sugar**

¾ **cup chocolate chips** *or* **chopped walnuts**

Preheat the oven to 350°F. Line two baking sheets with parchment paper. Position the racks in the upper and lower thirds of the oven.

Melt the chocolate in a medium heatproof bowl set directly in a wide skillet of barely simmering water. Stir frequently until the chocolate is almost completely melted, then remove from heat and stir to complete the melting. Set aside. (This can also be done in a microwave-safe bowl. Microwave in 20-second intervals, stirring between each, until chocolate is almost melted. The chocolate will continue to melt as it sits.)

In the bowl of a stand mixer fitted with the whisk or paddle attachment, beat egg whites with cream of tartar, vanilla, and salt until soft peaks form when you lift the beaters. Gradually add sugar, continuing to beat until stiff but not dry. Remove the beaters.

Pour warm chocolate and chocolate chips into the bowl; use a large silicone spatula to fold in until the batter is uniform. Immediately drop tablespoons of batter about 1 inch apart on prepared baking sheets. Bake for 8-10 minutes, or until the cookies look dry and feel slightly firm on the surface but are still gooey inside when you press on them.

Rotate the pans from top to bottom and from front to back halfway through the baking time to ensure even baking. Let the cookies cool for a few minutes on the baking sheets; then transfer to a rack to cool completely. The cookies are best on the day they are baked, but may be kept in an airtight container for 2-3 days.

HALVAH baklava

My all-time favorite stop in Machane Yehuda and in the new Sarona Market in Tel Aviv is Halva Kingdom. I think I have sampled all 60 flavors, or maybe that's just the dream. This business was founded in 1947 by the grandfather of the current shop owner, Eli Maman. After the expulsion of Jews from the Old City of Jerusalem, the family moved the shop to Machane Yehuda Market. The recipe of their famous halvah is from Morocco, and it is hand-made with traditional methods from organic sesame seeds imported from Ethiopia.

This recipe, with its addition of halvah to baklava, is another gem that I learned at Te'amim Cooking School in Jerusalem (see page 16). The richness that the halvah adds to the baklava is outrageous.

 YIELDS **10-12 SERVINGS**

PASTRY

15 sheets *(from a 1-pound box)* **phyllo dough,** *defrosted overnight in the refrigerator*

½ cup canola oil

FILLIING

1 cup roasted pistachios

1 cup roasted almonds

1 cup roasted pecans

1 pound halvah, *chopped*

2 teaspoons vanilla extract

HONEY SYRUP

½ cup sugar

½ cup honey

2 cups water

1 tablespoon lemon juice

Preheat the oven to 375°F. Line a jellyroll pan with parchment paper. Set aside.

Prepare the filling: Place the pistachios, almonds, pecans, halvah, and vanilla into the bowl of a food processor fitted with the metal "S" blade. Pulse until ground but not a paste. Set aside.

Prepare the syrup: Place the sugar, honey, water, and lemon juice into a medium pot. Over medium heat, bring to just a boil. Turn down to a simmer; cook for 10 minutes. Set aside.

Place a sheet of phyllo lengthwise on the work surface. Brush with canola oil. Top with another layer of phyllo. Brush with canola. Top with a third layer of phyllo and oil. Roll all four edges ½-inch inward to make a frame. Brush rolled edges with oil.

Spread a thick layer of the nut filling over the phyllo. Starting with a short end, roll up, jellyroll fashion; transfer to prepared sheet. Repeat, making 4 more rolled logs. Brush the logs with oil. Using a serrated knife, cut 4 diagonal slits across the top of each log.

Bake, uncovered, for 12 minutes, or until golden. Remove from oven and immediately spoon the syrup over the logs. Slice each log into 4-5 slices. Serve 2 slices to a plate. Drizzle with more syrup around the plate.

glazed DONUT twists

No need for donut envy when you see all the incredible photos of sufganiyot on social media all over Israel. And there is no need to wait for a Chanukah miracle to whip up these goodies! Another mighty fine option in place of the glaze is to toss twists while still warm into cinnamon-sugar.

 OR YIELDS **26-28 DONUT TWISTS**

DONUTS

2½ teaspoons instant *or* **bread machine yeast**

1 teaspoon *and* **¼ cup sugar,** *divided*

¼ cup warm water *(not too hot)*

1 stick *(8 tablespoons)* **butter** *or* **margarine,** *softened*

2 large eggs

¾ cup warm milk *or* **soymilk**

2 teaspoons fine sea salt

4 cups all-purpose flour, *divided, plus more for dusting surface*

canola oil, *for frying*

GLAZE

2 cups confectioner's sugar

¼ cup milk *or* **soymilk**

Place the yeast, 1 teaspoon sugar, and warm water into the bowl of a stand mixer fitted with the paddle attachment. Stir and allow to bubble, about 10 minutes. Add butter, ¼ cup sugar, eggs, ¾ cup milk, salt, and 2 cups flour. Beat until smooth. Add in remaining 2 cups flour and mix until a soft dough forms. Cover with a damp cloth; allow to rise in a warm place for 2 hours or overnight in refrigerator.

Line a cookie sheet with waxed paper or parchment paper. Punch the dough down. Divide the dough in half. On a lightly floured surface, roll one piece into a 9 x 11-inch rectangle. Cut widthwise into ¾-inch strips. Fold each strip in half lengthwise; twist 4-5 times. Pinch the ends to seal, place on prepared sheet. Repeat with remaining dough. Allow the donuts to rise while the oil heats.

Heat canola oil in a deep fryer or halfway up in a large pot, to 355°F. Fry the donuts, a few at a time, about 40 seconds per side until golden brown, using tongs to help turn them. Drain on paper towels. Return to cookie sheet to cool slightly.

Prepare the glaze: In a small bowl, combine confectioner's sugar and ¼ cup milk. Drizzle and brush over the donut twists.

new *fishbein* **BROWNIES**

My mother-in-law, Myrna Fishbein, was famous for her brownies. They were a rich, dense, fudgy chocolate. Kids used to write to her from summer camp because they knew the reward would be a box of these goodies. Purim meant that my husband and his dad would whip up dozens of batches. Fishbein Brownies have even been credited with saving the life of an Israeli soldier who left his base to pick up his care package of brownies and just missed being in an attack.

Over the years, times have changed, availability of brands have changed, and I have fiddled with the recipe, but I can think of no better end to the Kosher by Design series than with this, an ode to my husband's history, an evolved version of a simple, yet always satisfying, sweet, happy ending.

 D OR **P**   YIELDS **12 SERVINGS**

8 ounces best-quality semisweet chocolate, *broken into chunks*

1 teaspoon espresso powder *or* instant coffee granules

2 sticks *(1 cup)* unsalted butter *or* margarine

1⅓ cups all-purpose flour

1 teaspoon baking powder

1½ tablespoons Dutch process cocoa powder

¾ teaspoon fine sea salt

1¾ cups sugar

4 large eggs, *at room temperature*

2 teaspoons pure vanilla extract

Preheat the oven to 350°F. Coat a 7 x 11-inch brownie pan with nonstick cooking spray. Lay 2 strips of parchment paper into the pan to make a plus sign (+) with 2 inches of overhang. Coat the parchment with cooking spray as well. This will allow you to remove the brownies from the pan to cut them neatly. Set aside.

Melt the chocolate and espresso powder with the butter in a microwave-safe bowl using 30-second increments, stirring after each until smooth. This can also be done in a double boiler over a pot of simmering water. Set aside to cool for 5 minutes.

In a medium bowl, whisk together flour, baking powder, cocoa, and fine sea salt.

In a second bowl, whisk together sugar, eggs, and vanilla until they are a pale yellow. Slowly whisk in the melted chocolate. Whisk until thick and glossy. Stir in the flour mixture. Use a wooden spoon or silicone spatula to mix until smooth. Transfer to prepared pan.

For truly fudgy brownies, bake for 30 minutes. The top will be shiny. No need to stick a skewer in; the brownies will be too gooey to test. Immediately transfer from the oven to the refrigerator. If you like cakier brownies, bake for 45 minutes. Allow to become completely cold before serving.

INDEX

NOTES

  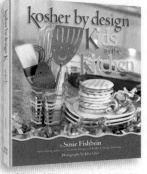 
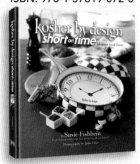 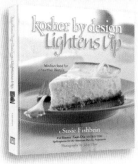 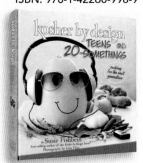